Kosher Fox

It all began for me one day when I was giving a talk on Jews and Jazz to a group. Someone came up to me and told me how Nat Temple had been the bandleader at their wedding. Trying not to look like an idiot, as I had never heard of Nat Temple, I mumbled something congratulatory and moved on, embarrassed. Why had I never heard of him?

As soon as I could, I looked up Nat Temple and his biography opened up a whole new world to me of Jewish bandleaders, and a forgotten Jewish history.

I read about people like Bert Ambrose and Harry Roy who when they died in 1971 were the forgotten men – Ambrose was the manager of a singer called Kathy Kirby, and mostly in retirement, and Harry Roy, four years the younger, had squandered a fortune, and was playing with a five-piece Dixieland Trad Jazz Band in Brighton.

Yet at one time I learnt they had been superstars. They had been A-list celebrities. Every household of every class and walk of life knew who they were, and would flock to get a glimpse of them.

They were part of a dance craze in Britain which lasted through the 1920s and 1930s called the "Golden Age of British Dance", a uniquely British art form with its roots in music hall and ballroom dancing, although influenced by jazz and swing.

In that era, dance bands (often called dance orchestras) abounded in the UK, and the earnings of the bandleaders matched that popularity - Harry Roy stated that his earnings in the 1930s were over £3,000,000 per year in today's money.

It lasted until the '40s and '50s, when the influence of Goodman, Armstrong, and Ellington could no longer be denied, and as musical tastes changed, those in or leading bands or orchestras who couldn't adapt to new styles of music, or refused to change, or simply weren't good enough, had had their day. It was change or die.

So for 20 years, British dance went in a markedly different direction from the U.S.A. and it was glorious while it lasted.

What I found surprising is that many of the band and orchestra leaders were Jewish – and so to remind people of the people and the time they lived their lives in, I wrote this book.

This book is their story.

Tony Zendle 2020/2021

Acknowledgements, credits and sources

The appendix at the back of this book shows the sources of much of my material. However, thanks to the many people who told me their stories of the dance bands, especially Yitz Jaffe of Cheadle.

My thanks, as with any of my books, go especially to my daughters Judith and Miriam, who did a big job proofreading and put up with my literary foibles, and my wife Liz who put up with the strains of Ambrose and Geraldo echoing through the house. Thanks, too, to David and Nicola who gave me advice, and listened to various ramblings.

Thanks too to Mum and Dad for the genes and the memories.

Notes

In Today's Money (ITM)

It is very difficult to equate today's money with the money that the bandleaders used to earn or with prices etc in the 1930s, so I have 'converted' the amounts from the 1920s and the 1930s to 2020. It is an inexact science but gives an idea of the scale of things. For example, Ambrose was quite happy to lay bets of £2,000 in the 1930s. A large amount nowadays, but when the conversion takes place, it becomes £130,000 which I signify as £130,000 ITM – In Today's Money, which gives a better representation of the excessive nature of his gambling than a mere £2,000.

If you think that cannot be true, you could get a loaf of bread for £0.01 in 1935, roughly equivalent to £0.90 ITM, and even as late as 1960 fish and chips cost £0.05 (compared to about a fiver nowadays).

Scotland, Wales, and Northern Ireland

I mention them rarely for the reason that I have not been able to find evidence of a Jewish bandleader coming from these countries. This is not to say that there were not glittering ballrooms in Belfast, Cardiff, Glasgow etc which were visited on a regular basis. Indeed, we have this cutting from 1953:

…and before we start, this book is dedicated to Liz:

You're the cream in my coffee
You're the salt in my stew
You'll always be my necessity
I'd be lost without you
You're the starch in my collar
You're the lace in my shoe
You'll always be my necessity
I'd be lost without you

Most men tell love tales
And each phrase dovetails
You've heard each known way
This way is my own way

You're the sail of my love boat
You're the captain and crew
You'll always be my necessity
I'd be lost without you

Source Unknown

Bandleaders' orchestra L-R Violins. Bert Ambrose, Joe Loss, Maurice Winnick, Sydney Lipton. Front Row. Roy Fox Trumpet, Harry Roy Clarinet, Billy Ternany Alto Sax, Lew Stone Piano. Early 1950s. Out of these eight top bandleaders, six are Jewish.

The amazing Joe Loss. Photo by Unknown Author is licensed under CC BY-SA-NC.

Addendum

Since I wrote the book, and began giving talks on the subject I have found that there is hardly a household in Britain that does not have a link with either the pre-World War II dance craze or the post-War Jazz revival in the UK.

I have been directed to various artists, sometimes great uncle, a distant relative, or a family friend.

In some cases as with Max Goldberg, they were sidemen, and highly talented, or as with Harry Klein or Vic Ash, from the Jazz era (maybe there's another book to be written), or as with Sidney Torch, a composer, pianist, and orchestral conductor.

What follows then is specifically about dance band leaders, their life and times. It is not a discography. It is a history.

Contents

CHAPTER 1: IN THE BEGINNING 11

THE GOLDEN AGE OF BRITISH DANCE 11
MUSIC, MAESTRO PLEASE 15
THE MUSIC HALL TRADITION 17
WHY NOT JAZZ? 17
WHAT ABOUT THE JEWS? 20

CHAPTER 2 - THE BIG FOUR 23

Bert Ambrose 23
Lew Stone 28
Geraldo 33
Harry Roy 41

CHAPTER 3 - SURVIVORS 51

Nat Temple 51
Joe Loss OBE 54
Oscar Rabin 57

CHAPTER 4 - CHANGING TRACKS 61

Sid Phillips 61
Woolf Phillips 62
Stanley Black OBE 64

CHAPTER 5 - MINOR BANDLEADERS 67

Benny Freedman 67
Benny Daniels 68
Benny Loban 70
Bert Firman 72
Sydney Lipton 74
Harry Leader 75
Sidney Simone 77

CHAPTER 6 - THE NORTHERN SET 79

North Manchester 79
Maurice Winnick 80
Nat Bookbinder 82
Johnny Rosen – The hard life 86
Phil Moss and the end of the Line 91

CHAPTER 7 - YIDDISHKEIT 95

    Assimilation and Dissimulation 95

    Jew-ish 97

    Jewish Music 100

    Summary 104

CHAPTER 8 - THE PHONE STOPS RINGING 105

APPENDIX 1 – SIDEMEN AND VOCALISTS 107

    Billy Amstell, Saxophone 107

    Alan Kane, Vocals 111

    Max Bacon, Drummer 112

    Harry Lewis 113

    Lew Davis, Trombonist 114

    Harry Gold 114

    Sam Browne. Vocalist 116

    Ray Ellington, Vocalist 117

    Charles 'Nat' Star, Recording Artist 118

APPENDIX 2 – THE ALBUM 123

APPENDIX 3 – "IZZY AZZY WOZZ" 125

APPENDIX 4 – WHEN HARRY MET GRACIE 127

APPENDIX 5 – THE TIME OF MY LIFE – EAMONN ANDREWS 133

APPENDIX 6 – THE BUSINESS OF THE DANCE BAND ERA 139

APPENDIX 7 - ARCHER STREET 149

APPENDIX 8 - JEWISH BRITJAZZ 157

BIBLIOGRAPHY/SOURCES 159

Copyright Tony Zendle

Caveat
I have attempted to verify facts from at least two separate and independent sources, but I take no ultimate responsibility for the verisimilitude of everything inside this book.

One thing to note. Occasionally the terminology is that of someone who grew up in North Manchester in the '60s. So, I write Shabbos, not Shabbat, or Sabbath. I write shool, not shul. Forgive me if it doesn't fit with your spelling.

Chapter 1: In the Beginning

The Golden Age of British Dance

By the turn of the 19th century, social dancing in the UK had developed to the point where old stylised group formation dances such as the polonaise and the gavotte had given way to dances such as the waltz, quickstep and foxtrot, where participants danced in couples.

It should be noted that one of the functions of the band that played aboard the Titanic in 1912 was to play at tea dances (for the First Class passengers) and that one of the last tunes heard as the ship was sinking was a waltz, *Song of Autumn.*

The likes of Irene and Vernon Castle and Victor Silvester helped to standardise the basic techniques of foxtrot, tango, quickstep and waltz, so by the mid-1920s, dance steps could be taught, and from then on, it wasn't just the top echelons in society that went dancing

As a result there was an almost exponential increase in the number of dance bands, and the increasing popularity of gramophone records and the radio, (and an accompanying decline in sales of sheet music.)

In the journal *Architectural History*, Dr James Nott of St Andrews University, an expert in the social history of dancing, wrote: "Highlighting the 'Craze for Dancing in London' in 1919, one newspaper remarked: 'London has gone dancing mad [...] dancing establishments in London are crowded morning, noon, and night with eager pupils [...] whilst dancing halls are booked up for months ahead.'"

Newspapers outside London also reported the enormous popularity of dancing. On its growth in northern English towns in 1920, the Cheltenham Chronicle commented: "Dancing, with 'the pictures' and football, fill in all the non-working hours in our great manufacturing towns, and, as a consequence, dancing masters not only teach the young how to step, but provide handsome dancing halls for them....."

Virtually all dance halls, right up to their decline in the 1960s, used live music, which would continue through the evening practically non-stop. The dance programme would usually last for four hours, during which about 50 dances were played. The bands were skilled at creating appealing programmes of music - varied, popular, and of the moment.

People flocked to the new dance halls, and the "glittering ballrooms" in smart hotels, restaurants and clubs, often for fun, but also for more down-to-earth reasons – that is, to meet a member of the opposite sex. Dennis Norden once said that it was "the only opportunity you got to get an armful of warm girl".

Some people reacted strongly against the dance halls:

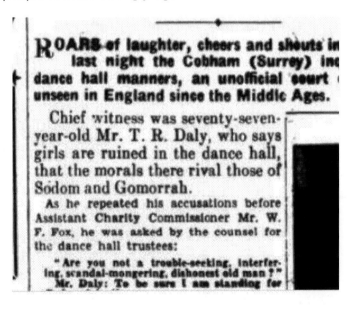

ROARS of laughter, cheers and shouts in last night the Cobham (Surrey) in dance hall manners, an unofficial court unseen in England since the Middle Ages.

Chief witness was seventy-seven-year-old Mr. T. R. Daly, who says girls are ruined in the dance hall, that the morals there rival those of Sodom and Gomorrah.

As he repeated his accusations before Assistant Charity Commissioner Mr. W. F. Fox, he was asked by the counsel for the dance hall trustees:

"Are you not a trouble-seeking, interfering, scandal-mongering, dishonest old man?"

Mr. Daly: To be sure I am standing for

Alternatively, a quote from a person who used to dance at the Brighton Regent is apposite: "Saturday night at the Regent was a must for us. It was an escape from reality for thousands of shop assistants, factory workers and employees who could afford to go out only once a week."

Bandleaders were the superstars of their time. In 1923, Ambrose's annual salary from just one hotel, the May Fair, was £600,000 (ITM), which is why he could afford to employ top musicians. Harry Roy claimed that at his peak he was earning £3,300,000 (ITM) per year, and would be paid £60,000 (ITM) to plug one of his records on the BBC for just one night.

Top bandleaders had regular spots on the radio with millions of listeners each week, and many of them also made recordings with leading record companies.

The most successful had a contract with a leading hotel in London, such as:

- The May Fair Hotel in Stratton Street
- The Embassy Club
- The Monseigneur Restaurant in Piccadilly
- The Savoy Hotel
- The Dorchester Hotel

.....and combining these with live radio was powerful: "Now ladies and gentlemen we take you over to the Monseigneur Club for Lew Stone and his Monseigneur Orchestra". The listener couldn't afford the prices at the Monseigneur Club, but he/she could be part of the experience.

In addition to the high-end venues, there were a plethora of dance halls to play at, from church halls to social clubs (such as working men's clubs). In Manchester and Liverpool, Lewis's Department Store restaurant on the 7th floor saw Johnny Rosen and his band playing at tea dances, while the staff canteen of the Ferguson Pailin

Engineering Works in Openshaw, Manchester could take hundreds of dancers, and even had a stage.

Here are just some of the venues around the country:

- Hammersmith Palais
- Blackpool Tower Ballroom (capacity a staggering 3,000)
- Manchester Ritz
- De La Warr Pavilion, Bexhill on Sea
- Palais de Danse, Nottingham
- Astoria Palais de Danse, Bolton
- The Liverpool Grafton Ballroom (capacity 1,200)

It is estimated that weekly attendance at these dances was four million, generating a revenue in today's terms of £1.5-2 billion per year. Big bucks.

Matching up the dance bands with the locations:

- Ambrose & His Orchestra and Harry Roy played at the May Fair Hotel in Stratton Street and subsequently at the Embassy Club in New Bond Street
- Roy Fox opened at the Monseigneur Restaurant in Piccadilly and subsequently appeared at the Café Anglais in Leicester Square and the Kit Kat Club in Haymarket
- Carroll Gibbons became closely associated with the Savoy Hotel, as did Geraldo and Fred Elizalde
- Joe Loss could be seen at the Astoria Ballroom in Charing Cross Road and the Hammersmith Palais
- Lew Stone and Mantovani played at the Monseigneur Restaurant in Piccadilly

As you can see, it was very London-centric, and why not? To be very successful, most bandleaders would need to have a residency at a London club, hotel, or dance hall at some time. Furthermore, it had big venues, it was the home of the recording studios, and it was the home of the BBC.

King Street Blues, an article written by Professor Kevin Morgan for Manchester University sums it all up:

"If today we think of the dance-band era, our likeliest images are those of dapper men with batons and their well-groomed orchestras, cocooning West End nightspots with their lulling arrangements. As one veteran put it, 'We were a typical society band of the 1930s, playing sweet music in a rather sedate manner, as required by the management, under soft lights in elegant surroundings.'

The bandleaders themselves, bearing suave and savvy names like Ambrose or Geraldo, seemed the very personification of musical escapism, a svelte divertimento in a world of constant discord. Even in their humbler manifestations, at local Mecca ballrooms where paste stood for diamonds, the dance bands' reflected musical ambience was that of Mayfair, conjuring away social barriers through the engulfing medium of radio."

Music, Maestro Please

A nice summary of the style that the bands played is from Wikipedia "British dance bands of this era typically played melodic, good-time music that had jazz and big band influences but also maintained a peculiarly British sense of rhythm and style which came from the music hall tradition."

This is correct but somewhat simplistic.

Dance band music tended to be classified as either "sweet" or "hot", often by the fans themselves. Ambrose and Geraldo were classified as "sweet", and Harry Roy was "hot". In the same way Glen Miller was "sweet" and Louis Armstrong and Duke Ellington were "hot"

This, too, is simplistic. Ambrose would often play "hot" and Harry Roy would play "sweet".

The point has been made that the people who came to the dances liked a judicious mix of the two styles; Fred Elizade, a brilliant musician, came a cropper at the Savoy when he attempted to play just one style,

Once again I am being simplistic, but "hot" tended to be in a jazz or swing style, that is with a degree of syncopation, and had clarinet or trumpet solos, and drums – whereas "sweet" was very melodic with piano or violin solos. "Sweet" was often better for mainstream dancing, and this is why, as we shall see later, Harry Roy often needed to keep his music "sweet"

Frustrated musicians would often find Jazz clubs to go to after their shift so they could play the music they really liked!

This is not to say that given the right circumstances British musicians could not have competed on the world stage with their compatriots in the USA. *Message from Mars*, composed by Sid Phillips and played by the Ambrose Orchestra is up there with the best, Lew Stone and *My Woman* with the vocal by Britains answer to Bing Crosby, Al Bowlly (who was tragically killed in the Blitz), has been described as a "snarling melody" and "sinister", and Harry Roys version of *Sugar Foot Stomp* by Louis Armstrong is transatlantic in the best sense of the word.

It is also noticeable that many Jazz standards were also released by British dance bands, although it has to be said that Lew Stones version of *Stars Fell on Alabama* pales in comparison with that produced by Satchmo and Ella Fitzgerald.

British musicians never really had the opportunities to fully take on board the tsunami that was swing, and were shielded from jazz influences. There is the story that when World War II began and American servicemen, fed on a diet of Benny Goodman, came to the dance halls of Liverpool and were played what was thought to be "hot" music, they jeered.

Jazz never really became part of the Golden Age, and for a number of reasons, which it is worthwhile to look at.

The music hall tradition

A small explanation.

Dance bands would often intersperse their acts with 'humorous' tunes such as *When Yuba Plays the Rumba on the Tuba*, *He Played His Ukulele as the Ship Went Down, Nobody Loves a Fairy When She's Forty, the* classic *My Girl's Pussy,* and the wartime *When Can I have a Banana Again.*

Quite often a member of the band would be singled out to give the comic tune, or vocalists brought on to perform, such as Max and Harry Nesbitt.

There were also variety numbers such as *Run, Rabbit, Run* that could be brought out of the cupboard when needed.

Why not jazz?

By the 1930s, celebrities such as Louis Armstrong, Duke Ellington and Benny Goodman were in (if you'll pardon the expression) full swing in the USA, yet in the UK, it took another 20 years for jazz to become mainstream. Instead jazz was relegated, as it is now, to specialist rhythm clubs.

There were four factors in this.

The first was protectionism in the shape of the Musicians' Union (MU), which was in a feud with its equivalent in the United States, the American Federation of Musicians (AFM). The MU had seen a reduction in membership after the advent of the 'Talkies' and the demise of the music hall. In the 1920s, if there was a vacancy in a British band, the job had first to be offered to a British player. The AFM responded by banning British musicians from the States.

In 1933, Duke Ellington appeared in the UK as part of a tour of Europe, but over the next 20 years, such luminaries as Louis Armstrong, Count Basie, and Benny Goodman were barred from playing in the UK. The MU was backed by the Ministry of Labour, so it took until 1958 for Ellington to play again in the UK. For many up and coming musicians these people would have been inspirational.

This protectionism was backed by the media. "In the 1920s the competition of foreign musicians was considered one of the main reasons for the difficulties experienced by musicians, especially those of a medium or low level. An article that appeared in the conservative newspaper Daily Express on 14th October 1925 clearly described how certain sectors of the population perceived the situation to be damaging for professional British musicians: The next musical invasion threatened is that of tango bands. Visiting the Musicians' Union, I found pavements of Archer street filled with unemployed bandsmen. There are over 500 out-of-work musicians in London; and yet foreign tango bands are seeking permits to come here, to play music which Englishmen can play equally well. "

Plus ca change. Tango this time, not Jazz, but the sentiments were the same no matter what the format.

The second factor was the attitude of people like the iconic controller of the BBC, Lord Reith, to the 'new music'. He detested the common man and his vulgarities, his litter, his "filthy jazz", and did not hesitate to proscribe what he did not like. Daughter Marista Leishmann's biography of Lord Reith tell us that he said: "Germany has banned hot jazz and I'm sorry that we should be behind in dealing with this filthy product of modernity."

Reith wasn't too keen on anything other than 'serious music' (meaning classical concerts, operas, symphonies and the like). As for a song such as *Love for Sale* (Cole Porter) - written from the viewpoint of a prostitute - ever being played on the BBC – ouch!

There was out-and-out racism too. In 1933 it was reported that a German (by which I assume they mean Jewish) conductor had employed "two coloured sax players" who were part of a "coloured band" at Ciro's Club in London. They were ultimately deported and replaced by a white band. Deported to where? They could have only come from the States!

Radio and jazz grew up at the same time. It is therefore little wonder that the types of music Reith allowed on the BBC were anodyne and non-jazzy. There can be no doubt that Reith saw jazz in the same way as the Germans did, as 'degenerate music'.

So jazz was kept from both the common man and the posh brigade, which is perhaps why the *Lambeth Walk* was more popular than *Take the A Train*.

The third reason, then. In the USA there was a vibrant black music scene which fuelled the development of jazz, with white musicians feeding into it. No such thing existed in the UK – there wasn't an ethnic minority with a base of ragtime and blues, so many white musicians in the UK never got exposed to the range of musical styles that their counterparts gained in the States.

As a fourth and final reason which I'll call separate development in the best sense of the phrase. Many bandleaders and musicians were well aware of jazz, and were not averse to playing it. However. Britain followed a different path from the USA, artistically – almost an alternate universe.

Jack Hylton called his music 'symphonic syncopation' It might have elements of Jazz in it, but it followed a British tradition of music hall, with light elements such as comedy and ballads interspersed. Harry Roy maybe came closer to jazz and swing, but his music was still peculiarly British, which after all is what the punters wanted. Jazz might be important, but it was still confined to private clubs. Dance music wasn't lesser than its American jazz counterpart. It was different, and followed a different tradition.

What about the Jews?

Quite a few of the bandleaders were Jewish – and what is more, many came from the East End of London or North Manchester.

And let me make this clear. They were not American, Dutch, French, Scottish, Welsh, or Irish. They were English (even if not born English). Also, the music they played conformed to Lord Reith's limited view of world music, which generally was not Jazzical (if I may be permitted to invent a word). Many of them became household names, some of them kept their faith, others didn't. Some had a long and glittering career. Others shone brightly and then disappeared.

The demographics of the time may explain why many Jewish bandleaders came from the East End or North Manchester. By 1914, the British Jewish population was estimated at 300,000, but 180,000 (two-thirds) of those were to be found in London, and 38,000 in Manchester and Liverpool. And of the 180,000 in London, 125,000 were in the East End.

To focus on the East End, it was logical that young Jews growing up in such a place as the East End would want to escape from the poverty. They were not sons of doctors or lawyers. They were the sons of immigrants who had a hard life, and they were looking for a form of escape.

They may have spoken Yiddish as a second language, but they had left the shtetl far behind, and they weren't interested in staying in the East End.

With the growth of mass entertainment, there were plenty of jobs in music halls, Yiddish theatre, cinemas in the East End paying next to nothing, but providing massive experience, and with the coming dance band craze post World War One, jobs were a plenty. If they could play an instrument, and play it well, and had a bit of ambition, the opportunities were there.

They all got started in different ways. Harry Roy just formed a band with his brother, Joe Loss's first professional engagements were at the local cinema where he would accompany the silent movies of the day, as did Gerald Bright (later to be known as Geraldo), as did Syd Lipton, as did Maurice Winnick. Phil Moss began with the Jewish Lads Brigade Bugle Band!

For Bernard Baruch Ambrose, who had learnt the violin, the opportunity arose when he was sent to the States to avoid the Zeppelins, and got a job with a dance band in a restaurant in New York. He said that he was thrown out of the band after a couple of weeks. Harry Roy's first job was with his brother at the Hammersmith Palais.

Billy Amstell's story in Appendix 1 gives an insight into how many got started, but they will have all had their own paths.

No matter how they began their careers, the more ambitious amongst them felt that they could do more – that they wanted the music to be played their way, and were not happy to just be a sideman to a band. So they started to lead the band, and a new phenomenon was born – the English Jewish Bandleader.

Also, because of the density of co-religionists, support mechanisms were on tap, especially in the East End and near London where the music publishers, record companies, and agents were located. Many of the publishers and agents were Jewish, and to have a record company on your doorstep was a distinct advantage.

They changed from being the children of immigrants to being part of the fabric of British life. Many of them became secular in outlook and left their roots far behind.

In North Manchester, it was the same as the East End. Perhaps they had less conveniently situated for the record companies, but the wish to escape was just as true in Prestwich as in Whitechapel.

It is now time to chronicle their lives.

Advertisement from the 1920s

Chapter 2 - The Big Four

There was talent aplenty, but four stood out from the pack – Bert Ambrose, Lew Stone, Geraldo, and Harry Roy. Their impact was such that any biography of those days is bound to mention them.

We need to start with…………

Bert Ambrose

In every musical generation, there are those that are exceptional. Ambrose was one such – not only for his abilities with the baton, but for the way he influenced a whole generation that followed him, and how he attracted the best musicians in the country to his band, which itself was recognised as the best in the country. To have played with Ambrose was to have him as a great reference on your curriculum vitae. He has been referred to as the dance band messiah.

To begin: living in Mile End, East London was a recent immigrant from Poland, one Louis Ambrose, a dealer in rags. He had a son. Benjamin Baruch Ambrose, born in Warsaw in 1896, who in the 1911 census was called Barnett. He was 14 years old and already called a violin musician, having left school (the school leaving age being 14 in 1911).

He went to New York around 1915 (he said in an interview that his mother wanted him to avoid the Zeppelins dropping bombs on London), and stayed for a number of years. He seems to have started playing with bands soon after arriving, for he soon had a job at Reisenweber's restaurant, which had a dance floor.

According to Ambrose the job lasted just a few weeks, but he found another band at the Palais Royal in Manhattan, where he had more success, going from, as he told the story, 6th violinist (out of six) to bandleader in just six months. He was 20.

He stayed in New York for a few years, coming back to London on occasion, and finally, after some shilly-shallying, began as bandleader at the Embassy Club in Mayfair in 1923. His time in New York had been well-used. The influences to which the young Bert Ambrose must have been exposed would have been several and numerous. Sophie Tucker was in cabaret, Al Jolson was a star on Broadway, and Paul Whiteman was in town, and when he finally returned to London in 1923, he was ready to become one of the top bandleaders in the country.

National Portrait Gallery Creative Commons

He stayed at the Embassy until 1927, but was tempted away by the May Fair Hotel, not only by the aforementioned £600,000, but also because he wanted to do radio work, and gain recording contracts.

While at the May Fair, he did two things. He began to employ only the best sidemen for his band, and he started to make records for HMV and Decca, not only for the UK market, but for the US too. In the States, he was the only bandleader to seriously challenge the home-grown talent.

During the summer months he would play at Monte Carlo, Cannes, and Biarritz. As was said by Julian Vedey "No playground of the rich was complete without Ambrose".

Some of the sidemen who played with him were the cream of the crop, such as Sid Phillips, George Chisholm, Henry 'Hot Lips' Levine, Nat Temple, Ted Heath, Stanley Black, Lew Stone. The list is (almost) endless. He was also not averse to playing straight jazz, as evidenced by his band's performance of *Deep Henderson*, a swing/jazz classic also played by the jazz great King Oliver.

He was no angel. He had at least one affair, with Evelyn Dall, one of his singers, which seemed to have lasted for years, and ended in 1953 according to the Daily Telegraph when he refused to divorce his wife.

He was a compulsive gambler, boasting that he had lost millions of pounds at the tables. Once, when in the south of France, he had to wire his London office for money to pay his musicians, and Cyril Stapleton, a fellow bandleader, told the story to Allan Dell that if the Aga Khan of those days bet £1,000 (£70,000 ITM) Ambrose would bet double that amount, to show how wealthy he himself was. The casino in Biarritz was nicknamed Chez Ambrose. He said that one evening at the tables in Monte Carlo he lost £180,000 ITM.

Why all of this? He came from poverty. Money was a means to him and not an end, and he said himself that if he lost a lot of money when gambling he would still sleep easily at night – but if the band played badly that was another matter.

Returning to the music, in the online *Dance Band Encyclopaedia*, it said: "Few, if anybody called him 'Bert'. He was called 'Mr. Ambrose' (or 'Ammy' by his friends)". He has been described as shrewd, quick-witted, fiery-tempered, with a mixture of dignity and offensiveness, and with a sardonic sense of humour. He used to insult the customers outrageously at the smart venues he played. He taunted his musicians with cruel comments but equally was quick to praise and when complimented on the excellence of the band, would acknowledge the musicians.

Stanley Black said: "The Ambrose band was looked on as some sort of a university; how to play in a dance band, a very good dance band."

Ambrose with Rogers and Hart – Wiki Commons -1927

He was very successful – on Desert Island Discs he told the story of how one evening he had nine orchestras playing under his name at private parties, and he also bought and opened a club called Ciros.

It was he that 'discovered', Vera Lynn, and she was with Ambrose and his Orchestra for three years, after she left Joe Loss.

Having said that, Lynn's obituary in the Daily Telegraph stated "She then graduated to the sophisticated Ambrose Orchestra, though Bert Ambrose at first used her only on a Radio Luxembourg show, sponsored by Lifebuoy toilet soap, until limited exposure on a BBC broadcast, when she was rationed to one song, started a flood of fan mail. Even then, Ambrose made it clear that he preferred his other female singer, the American Evelyn Dall."

However, it is true that Ambrose kickstarted Vera Lynn's career, and people such as Ronnie Scott, who was to lead British jazz in the '50s, played with him and learnt from him.

After the war, where Ambrose certainly did much less for the Forces than his fellow bandleaders Harry Roy and Geraldo, when dance bands went into decline, Ambrose semi- retired from bandleading.

Nick Dellow, in his Facebook page on the "Golden Age of Dance Bands group noted that "Ambrose, like many other dance band leaders, struggled after the Second World War, a situation not helped by his addiction to gambling. He opened with a new band at Ciro's Club on 8th October 1945 - a band that included many of the top musicians from the pre-war days, including Billy Amstell and Max Goldberg - but money was in short supply and business was slow for many West End nightspots. "

Nick referred to Bill Amstells autobiography *Don't Fuss, Mr Ambrose* where he said "Ambrose's engagement at Ciro's Club came to an abrupt end on 19th March 1947. This was near the end of the Big Freeze, when the music business in London's West End was severely hit by the weather. As we were on the bandstand ready to play to an empty room, Ambrose walked in looking downcast and spotting Captain Nathan at his table on the balcony, joined him. In the silence of the room we heard 'Ammy' say, "You don't need us here, Nathan, do you?" "Not really," came the reply.

And so we finished. The dance band days as I had known them for the previous 20 years had finished also, though I may not have realised it at the time. It was the end of a golden era; The Golden Age Of The Dance Bands, as it has so often been called.

Ambrose returned to London's West End again in 1948-49, leading a band at the Nightingale Club, but things really went downhill for him as a bandleader from then on in; in the 1950s he was reduced to touring around the country by coach to fill one-night stands."

He went into management, managing a singer called Kathy Kirby, with whom it is intimated that he was having an affair. That did not have a good ending as Kirby's career too went into decline, partially, as the Independent stated, because "Ambrose's managerial arrogance and old-fashioned values so annoyed BBC and ITV executives that TV appearances had petered out by 1970".

He died in 1971 in Leeds while on business, and is buried in Bushey Cemetery, Middlesex. According to Amstell, around 30 musicians, and one relative went to the funeral. At one time it would have been thousands.

Lew Stone

The Jewish Museum chose three bandleaders amongst those who have been the most influential in the arts in the UK.

One was Lew Stone.

Lew Stone was born Louis Steinberg in Bethnal Green in 1898, the son of a cabinetmaker. By the time he was 29 he had become known as a top-class arranger and was employed by Bert Ambrose to write arrangements for him.

What happened next depends on which version you read.

In one version: "By 1931, Stone was working with Roy Fox in Piccadilly, enchanting audiences from the stage of the Monseigneur Restaurant. Stone stepped into the leader's position the following year, when Fox decided to move on."

In another tale: "Lew Stone, having already made a name for himself as a craftsman of snappy arrangements... found himself in charge when the bandleader Roy Fox fell ill."

In a third: "Fox fell ill with pleurisy and travelled to Switzerland for a stay at a sanatorium. During his convalescence the band was led by its pianist, Lew Stone.

Upon his return he was unable to agree terms with the Monseigneur Restaurant, and the owners offered the residency to Stone .... and all the band with the exception of trumpeter Sid Buckman decided to remain with Stone. Fox took out an injunction on the grounds of breach of contract against his singer Al Bowlly .....but Fox lost his action."

Origin unknown

History is written on behalf of the victor, and whereas Lew Stone had the look of your favourite uncle, Louis Steinberg came from a tough environment and it was dog eat dog. His band also knew what side their bread was buttered on, and didn't make waves.

Consolidating his position, the music Stone then brought to the Monseigneur's dance floor made the band so popular that he was given the job permanently.

He had the good luck that Bowlly had been with Fox, and took Bowlly's work to new levels. Their partnership helped the band eventually to be ranked amongst the best in London, and Stone furthered his career by making recordings with Decca and radio broadcasts on the BBC.

He was clearly a man of many talents, pianist, cellist, arranger, bandleader, but what makes him stand out was that at a time when dance bands were producing anodyne music for the minority upper class audiences, it was he, through his recording of such tunes as *White Jazz*, who laid the groundwork for the later jazz explosion in the UK in the '50s.

Humphrey Lyttleton said: "There has long been a myth that, when it came to jazz, British dance musicians were a square and clueless breed. You have only to hear the affection with which Nat Gonella flattered Louis Armstrong's style, or the way in which Lew Davis mastered the plunger trombone techniques originated by Duke Ellington's players, to realise that enthusiasm for jazz was rife in the Lew Stone band".

Source unknown. Lew Davis (see Appendix) is to the right of Lew Stone. Al Bowlly to the left.

He was lucky, too, that he met his life partner Joyce at the Monseigneur. She was a debutante, and at her 21st birthday party, and he was from the East End and in his late thirties, but seemingly they hit it off straight away. She went on to support him all his life, taking the administrative burden off him, and although not Jewish (which given her class, and the anti-Semitism of the time must have caused some problems), became a massive supporter of Israel, and a Jewish National Fund benefactor. She also became somewhat of an expert on the Golden Age, and was a consultant to the BBC when they filmed Dennis Potter's *Pennies from Heaven*".

Stone moved around the hotels, at one point having Alan Kane (the son of a cantor) as his vocalist, and during the war years toured the country. He was never really out of work, residing at various places, including the Pigalle, and as time went on he moved increasingly into swing and jazz.

As for his personal life, Stone was an enigma. Biographies of him do not expose the inner man. He married an upper middle-class person who didn't conform to the stereotype. He was a committed socialist , and became involved with the anti-war People's Convention during the early part of World War II.

The People's Convention was initially a front for the Communist Party, blaming the war on imperialism/capitalism, and calling for a people's government that would overthrow the ruling classes and help workers in Germany rise to defeat Hitler. Naïve at the very least, it had a certain appeal for a while, but was strongly opposed by the Labour Party and the unions. It died the death after 1941, especially when the Communist Party withdrew its support after Hitler's invasion of Russia, but the Stones (and Kane) were early signatories, and Lew Stone was on an organising committee.

This showed maybe that despite having been, as it were, fed and watered by the "upper classes" at the posh restaurants where he played, Stone maybe had kept some of the radicalism of his youth.

He was banned, amongst others, by the BBC for having been a signatory, but this ban was reversed after intervention by Winston Churchill who was under significant pressure to do so. Three days after the reversal of the ban, Germany invaded the Soviet Union, and the War was no longer an 'Imperialist War'.

Considering the views of the Jewish community at the time, Stone clearly swam against the tide, and seemed to distance himself even further from his Jewish roots.

During the War, his music would once again be banned by the BBC, but because it was felt to be too 'American' (swing being anathema to the BBC). However, it is noted that his band toured the aerodromes and army camps, on one occasion some of his audience walked out, not because they disliked his political views, but because they were off to bomb the Great Dams of Germany, as they were 617 squadron (The Dambusters)!

After the war, he slowly gave up bandleading and went into management. One can understand that. The Golden Age was over, and few survived.

He died in 1971. He had been an innovator at a time when innovation was frowned upon.

Geraldo

Geraldo was a shapeshifter, a chameleon.

He was born Gerald Walcan Bright in Islington in 1904, the son of Isaac Bright, a rag merchant/tailor, and twin brother to Sydney. Both he and Sydney seem to have been gifted, for it is noted that they studied music at the Royal College of Music, but neither were destined for a classical career.

Gerald played piano at local cinemas to accompany silent films, but then 'ran away to sea', something that would come in very useful later in life when he organised bands for Cunard.

In an interview in 1969 with Tony Brown, he said: "I ran away to sea when I was 16-and-a-half and joined the orchestra on the *Cameronia*. We went to New York and I was scared out of my wits. I'd never been away from home before. It broke my mother and father's heart. They were very hurt about it, but it was my salvation, really.

I asked them to let me go and they wouldn't, so I left. When I went to Charlie Black in Liverpool to get a job he said: 'How old are you?'

I told him I was 21-and-a-half. 'Have you got a passport?' asked Charlie. I hadn't, so he told me to go and get one. I went into a Commissioner for Oaths along the road and asked him to fill in the form for me. I told him I was over 21 and he signed the form and sent it off.

It was the greatest move I could have made. It gave me a sense of responsibility and taught me to stand on my own feet and think for myself."

Returning to land, his career took an unusual step, for unlike his contemporaries, he didn't look for work in one of the London café or hotel dance bands but made the decision to go up North, where the music scene was perhaps less crowded.

The decision must have been made easier, as he was estranged from his parents. He used his talents as a pianist at the Tower Ballroom in Blackpool, forming his own band in 1922 at the Hotel Metropole and then playing from 1925 at The Majestic Hotel in St Anne's as Gerald Bright and His Majestic Celebrity Orchestra.

He stayed there for five years, and gained an audience by broadcasting on BBC Northern region three times a week – and then moved to London, where it seems he reinvented himself after what has been described as a 'visit' to Argentina.

When Rudolph Valentino, dressed as a gaucho, delivered a sultry tango in *The Four Horsemen of the Apocalypse* (1921), it attracted millions more adherents, and in the 1920s and 1930s the tango became a socially acceptable dance. Dance bands latched on to this new fad, and none more so than Gerald Bright from Islington, who became Geraldo and, with his pencil moustache and his dark, Latin looks, formed what has been described as the "distinctly inauthentic Geraldo's Gaucho Tango Orchestra".

He wasn't the only one latching on to this trend. Ambrose was occasionally billed as the "Latin from Mayfair" (rather than Poland, if you see what I mean).

There was, of course, Bertini (of Blackpool Tower Ballroom Dance Orchestra fame), whose real name was Bert Gutsell, Alfredo (Alfred Gill), and Waldini (Wally Bishop). Anything to make a living, but they did not have the same chameleon-like quality as Geraldo.
He took up residence at the Savoy Hotel in 1930, began making recordings, appeared at the Royal Command Performance in 1933, and his career was made.

He could spot the end of a trend. In a Pathé film in 1934, there is *Geraldo and his Sweet Music.* Instead of gaucho outfits, he and his band are wearing tuxedos. A complete change of sound as well.

By this time, he had become musical director for Herbert Wilcox, the well-known producer at Elstree Studios and Pinewood during the 1930s.

The band was highly successful, and as with Ambrose, during the summer season, followed the wealthy to their holiday locations in the South of France. Julien Vedey puts that success down to two factors:

Firstly, his band had a wide repertoire – they would play hit tunes, samba, rumba, waltz, swing – there was always something the audience liked. Secondly, he knew how to 'play' an audience – quite often he would get them to sing a well know song. Almost unimaginable to think of Ambrose doing that.

It is clear that he was a driven man. His early life shows someone driven by ambition – he walked out on his family, moved away from his beginnings, and took opportunities where they lay.

Band members of his were somewhat circumspect about his character.

Ivor Mairants (guitar):

"Geraldo was never one of the boys and never one of the people. He was very polite but he never had the warmth.

We were playing the Newcastle Empire when Ted Heath told Geraldo that he wanted to start his own band and gave him two weeks' notice. Gerry was angry and told him to leave right there and then and pay his own fare back. When Gerry hated, he hated."

Harry Gold

"Geraldo never rehearsed because he expected you to read perfectly first go and if you couldn't you were out immediately."

Nat Temple

"Geraldo had an enormous number of contacts and knew how to pull strings... he played piano but not very well... in spite of his reputation he was the shyest person imaginable. When he was on stage, he would never look at the audience."

Be careful about reading too much into this. Geraldo was not universally popular with his sidemen, but he wasn't in the business of being loved. He had character flaws, but he also had massive success.

His activities during World War II deserve some mention. As with most of the bandleaders he was highly patriotic, and he certainly played his part. From the beginning of the war, there was deep suspicion of anyone who wasn't in the services. Notwithstanding that, around 80% of band personnel joined up, leaving those who had medical problems or were too old. Although there was need to entertain the troops and the home workers, musician was not a reserved occupation, and it has been noted that singers especially were seen as some sort of unpatriotic lounge lizard.

The truth was that the dance bands did an amazing job to keep up the morale in the country, and were just as important for the war effort as any other form of entertainment such as film and radio, and Geraldo was at the forefront.

David Tunley said "The war years called upon his gifts and boundless energy as never before. In a short article in the Radio Times of February 1942 he was said to have completed that week thirteen stage appearances, nine broadcasts, five factory shows, and about a thousand miles of travel.

The Geraldo Concert Orchestra put together for ENSA consisted of his usual dance band plus members from the London Symphony Orchestra".

ENSA was of course the Entertainments National Service Association, which was set up "to provide entertainment for British armed forces personnel". Quality was variable – it had the soubriquet Every Night Something Awful, and Geraldo was brought in to be musical director, with the aim of making improvements.

It was during this period in January 1942 that Geraldo had a spat with Malcolm Sargent on the BBC show *Brains Trust*, when it was discussing "Is Vera Lynn harmful to morale?" and Sargent claimed swing was inferior to classical. Geraldo suggested that they swap batons to prove that dance musicians had as high a standard of technical ability and musicianship as classical players.

Original wartime caption: Geraldo and his orchestra with singers visited an RAF desert airfield and gave a show in the open-air. The stage consisted of boards resting on empty oil drums. The dressing room for the artists was a three-ton truck and the gallery was the roofs of trucks and lorries. After the show Geraldo said it was one of the best audiences he had ever had.

Together with Jack Payne's band his was the house band for the BBC, serving for three years, but this was brought to an end in January 1944 when he was sacked by the BBC. It was felt that his music was too American, something that Harry Roy had an argument with the BBC about both before and after Geraldo's sacking.

The timing was rotten. He had just finished a highly successful tour of the Middle East, and his popularity amongst the troops was massive, not least because he retained some of his North London accent. They felt that he was one of them.

Vis-à-vis his accent, there is the apocryphal story that King George, when presented to Geraldo (at the time of his Gaucho Band) at the Royal Variety performance was somewhat surprised when Geraldo opened his mouth and (instead of Buenos Aires) out came Islington.

Notably in 1943, he appeared in a film called "We'll Meet Again" as "Gerry", the bandleader, in what was a showcase for Vera Lynn.

As can be seen from the screenshot above, he had, by this time completely shed his dark Latin looks (and the moustache)

After the war, with his band still in operation he acted as agent for the shipping lines Cunard and Canadian Pacific to recruit musicians for the entertainment of passengers on the. regular transatlantic crossings as well as cruises to the West Indies and world cruises.

Thus Cunard became known as Geraldo's Navy. Amongst the many musicians that were members of Geraldo's Navy was one Ronald Schatt, later to be known as Ronnie Scott, the famous night club owner.

Kenny Harris, who wrote a book called Heraldo's Navy said "Many of the musicians who signed up for Geraldo in the late 1940s were jazz enthusiasts who wanted to get to New York to hear the 'new' bebop of Charlie Parker, Dizzy Gillespie and others live in the clubs.

There were no records available in the UK so the musicians could bring back records and other difficult to obtain musical items."

Geraldo died in 1974 on holiday in Switzerland, and is buried at Willesden Jewish Cemetery.

What of his twin brother? Sydney Bright remained true to the Jewish faith, becoming choirmaster at the North London Synagogue in Islington. He never became a bandleader, but worked with Jack Hylton, Caroll Gibbons, and interestingly enough, his brother.

When Geraldo died, I guess it was Sydney who made all the arrangements. He died two years after his brother.

Summing up, Geraldo – he was probably the cleverest of all of them, and certainly the most astute businessman.

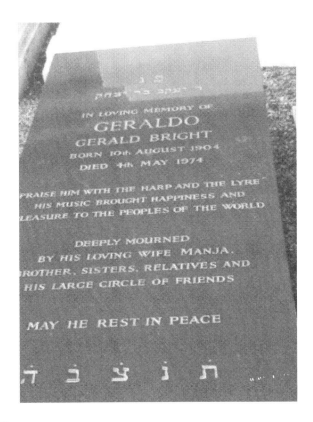

Harry Roy

Harry Roy was the showman, the exact opposite of the sophisticated Ambrose, whom he followed at the Mayfair Hotel from 1934-1936. One might say that where Jack Hylton was the brains behind the dance band revolution, Roy was the beating heart.

He understood that publicity was everything and that the media offered opportunities, in a way that the other bandleaders did not recognise – if it wasn't Harry Roy playing in a charity cricket match, it was Roy carrying his band's golf clubs, or playing in a charity football match, or getting married, or flying off on his holidays.

Harry Roy, Baby, Wife and Band Off to South America

He appeared in two movies as well (with his first wife) and although his acting was of variable quality, they didn't 'bomb'.

However, those that live by the sword, die by the sword, and the publicity wasn't always favourable

'Lucky Ted'

BANDLEADER Harry Roy, who has had more than his fair share of bad luck since the golden days when he earned £1,000 a week—and lost £72,000 in one racing season—is keeping his fingers crossed

For he has at last achieved his ambition to join the ranks of Mayfair night club owners. Next month he is opening Harry Roy's Femina—and Roy, who has lost several fortunes in unfortunate business ventures, knows that competition in the Mayfair jungle is tough.

HARRY ROY REVEALS HIS SECRET ROMANCE

HARRY ROY the dance band leader, is to marry Sonia Stacpoole, 27, former showgirl who became dancer and singer in his band.

The wedding will take place at Caxton Hall, London, soon It has been kept so secret that Harry's band knew nothing about it.

Born as Harry or Harris Lipman in Stamford Hill in 1900, he initially worked for his father, Solomon Lipman. We are told that it wasn't until he was 16 that he began to learn the clarinet and sax, and thus was a late starter – by 16 years of age, Bert Ambrose was in New

York playing in restaurants, and Gerald Bright was playing piano on cruise liners, but as with everything Harry went his own way.

He teamed up at age 21 with his brother Sydney. Sydney led the band initially, and the band must have been pretty good, because by 1922 it was playing at the Hammersmith Palais de Danse.

They came to be known as Syd Roy's Lyricals, and were highly successful over the next few years; as far as I can tell Harry played the comedian for the band, and there were many changes of personnel (not unusual for those days).

Towards the end of the 1920s the band went on a World Tour, and then to Germany in 1930, where the Dance Band Encyclopaedia states that the band "effectively broke up". Another biography in the Allmusic website states that the band "fell apart". One feels that there may have been tensions about musical direction, and maybe Syd's leadership.

The Dance Band Encyclopaedia takes up the story: "In 1931, Syd Roy was asked to form a big band for the new RKO Theatre in Leicester Square. He decided it needed someone dynamic with a strong personality to front the band, so he asked his brother, setting him on the road to fame.

After this, Syd increasingly wound down his bandleading duties and became Harry's manager."

Over the next few years, Harry showed that he had what it took – taking over from Syd and playing at various top venues such as the Alhambra and the London Coliseum, and touring South Africa, Australia and Germany.

By the time we get to 1930, Harry Roy had climbed to the top of the tree, and his best years were yet to come - recording, performing on radio (notably from the Café Anglais in 1933, where his twice weekly broadcasts brought in 2,000 fan letters a week) and having a residency at the Mayfair Hotel.

The reason for his success is clear. He provided the public with an alternative to bland. At one point he was a greater pull than any of his contemporaries, topping the bill at variety theatres all over Britain. He was described as an energetic livewire on stage with a Jolson-like voice. Heavily influenced by the styles of the American performers Cab Calloway and Ted "Mr Entertainment" Lewis, he was quite happy to engage in scat singing in the style of Satchmo. One biography has him down as a "born showman, comedian, and vocalist".

He had not gone straight into the café world, but in 1933 he took over Ambrose's residency at the May Fair hotel. In the book *Talking Swing: The British Big Bands* by Sheila Tracey, she states "When the band was booked to play in the May Fair in 1933 sceptics from Tin Pan Alley to Archer Street predicted disaster. No way would the upper crust of London Society accept this scat singing, clarinet tooting rowdy showman. How wrong they were. It wasn't long before Harry Roy had the May Fair clientele eating out of his hand".

Julian Vedey in his book *Bandleaders* noted "The bright young things of May Fair took him to their hearts with an affection equal to that of the jive crazy bobbysox".

The photograph below demonstrates Harry Roy at his best.

Copyright Pathé

He was also well known for writing songs with suggestive lyrics, notably *My Girl's Pussy,* and *She Had to Go and Lose It at the Astor.* Roy never went too far, though. He may have recorded *Tiger Rag*, a "hot" tune, but he was careful not to upset the patrons of the May Fair.

Nat Temple, who worked in Harry Roy's band, summed it up: "The May Fair was very posh indeed. We played sotto voce because in those days people insisted on that so that they could carry on talking while they were dancing past the band without having to raise their voices.

That was essential. You must play quietly. The clientele were the aristocracy. You didn't take much notice of whether they were dukes or earls, they were just there with their funny evening dress."

Roy went wherever the work was – as a recording artist or on tour to South Africa, Australia, Paris – wherever anyone wanted to hear his work. With his wife, he even starred in a film called *Everything is Rhythm*.

He was earning massive amounts, he estimated to be the equivalent of £3,500,000 (ITM) – he stated would earn £30,000 a night (ITM) from records companies for plugging their records on the BBC.

He lived the high life – he estimated that by 1939 he had lost a quarter of a million gambling on the horses – a lot of money even these days! In 1935 he married Elizabeth Brooke, daughter of the last white Rajah of Sarawak, Sir Charles Vyner de Windt Brooke, with mink coats and gold cigarette cases being given as presents, and honeymooning in Nice.

In 1939 he had the first of his arguments with the BBC, who wanted to choose which numbers he played for them – he won out in the end.

Then came the war. He joined ENSA, and pretty soon went to France with Vera Lynn in 1940. Later with a small band which he called Harry Roy's Tiger Ragamuffins he went to the Middle and Far East, as well as playing in nightclubs.

He had a final big bust up with the BBC in 1944.

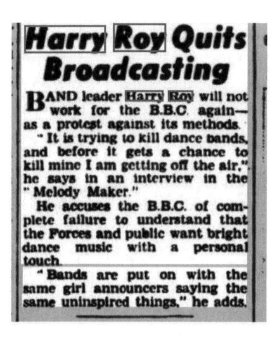

Harry Roy Quits Broadcasting

BAND leader Harry Roy will not work for the B.B.C. again—as a protest against its methods.

" It is trying to kill dance bands, and before it gets a chance to kill mine I am getting off the air," he says in an interview in the " Melody Maker."

He accuses the B.B.C. of complete failure to understand that the Forces and public want bright dance music with a personal touch.

" Bands are put on with the same girl announcers saying the same uninspired things," he adds.

They later made it up, and one might have expected that post-war, things would look up for Roy, with the increasing interest in jazz and swing, but life didn't work out as he expected.

His marriage fell apart in 1947. Nat Temple said "he was a little unfaithful and the marriage broke up", and in 1948 he was refused a work permit by the USA because the American Federation of Musicians stated that a condition of the permit was that the person had to have been resident in the USA for six months. It was blatant protectionism, and Roy was forced to return. Every cloud has a silver lining, though, for on return to Britain, he reformed his band and scored a hit with his recording of *Leicester Square Rag*.

He also remarried, this time to Sonia Stacpoole, a Windmill dancer. But *Leicester Square Rag* in 1949 was his last big hit. The game was over for Harry. His style, which was new and fresh in the 1930s, was outdated and pathetic for the Rock 'n Rollers in the 1950s, and the money wasn't there anymore. He never established himself with the new jazz generation, driven by Ronnie Scott and Chris Barber – his roots were elsewhere.

He is credited as being on the very first episode of *Come Dancing* as a musician, but never took advantage of the opportunities of the TV age, unlike others of his generation such as Nat Temple. Given his penchant for vaudeville this is surprising, but as we have seen he had an ability to rub people up the wrong way, so maybe no offers were made.

As said, he had had his time. For example, *Leicester Square Rag* is fun, the musicianship is excellent, the melody is good......and it belongs to the 1930s.

Like many, he struggled on, but after a while he had had enough, and bought a restaurant. After it burned down, he tried to restart his career, but by then he was in bad health, and it was all too late.

As mentioned he ended his days playing in a Trad Jazz Band in Brighton. When interviewed in 1971 he said that he was very contented; he had become bored with the high life - but for someone who had been at the very core of the dance band movement, life, in the end, must have been a disappointment.

He died later that year. Jack Trevor Storey said that when Harry Roy passed away, so did a whole era.

Chapter 3 - Survivors

The war years changed everything.

Many bandleaders joined the Services. After the war some made the decision to change careers. They wanted to be finished with the punishing schedule that light entertainment demanded. Maybe, as with Geraldo, they left to be their own boss.

Furthermore, the wave upon wave of U.S. servicemen coming to these shores, bringing jazz, swing, and blues with them was to transform British culture forever.

As was noted by Roberta Schwartz: "Imported recordings of American artists were brought over by African American servicemen stationed in Britain during and after World War II, by merchant seamen visiting the ports of London, Liverpool, Newcastle on Tyne and Belfast, and in a trickle of (illegal) imports."

To young people dance bands with their conductors dressed in "penguin suits" were an anachronism. To put it in the vernacular of the time "It's Trad, Dad".

Some bandleaders, however, never fell out of fashion. They changed with the times. Nat Temple and Joe Loss had careers that were remarkable for their amazing longevity. One feels that Oscar Rabin, too, would have lasted the course, but sadly he died relatively young.

Nat Temple

Nat Temple was almost unique in that he made the transition from dance band to light entertainment with ease, and when he died there was an outpouring of grief; obituaries in all the main papers as well as the trade papers. Whereas with the other bandleaders, you felt they may have been respected or admired, this man was loved.

It was simply that everyone who met him liked him. He had a great sense of humour, was self-deprecating, really well organised, but was not a driven man in the same way that Ambrose, Geraldo or Roy were. Moreover, he was recognised as a man of serious talent, playing the clarinet and alto-saxophone at the highest level.

He was born in Stepney in 1913, son of a tailor. At the age of 18 he joined Syd Lipman's band, which was a good move, as Syd was Harry Roy's brother. By the '40s, he had already worked with such luminaries as Harry Roy, Geraldo, Ambrose, and Lew Stone.

As stated, he was a natural clarinettist, and according to his obituary in the *Daily Telegraph*: "In later life Temple revealed that he himself had played most of the clarinet solos on Harry Roy's records in the 1930s, and been well paid to do so and keep quiet about it.

"He was, however, reputed to be the first British clarinettist to successfully execute the difficult opening glissando of Gershwin's *Rhapsody in Blue*".

He may have gone on just being a sideman to bands and orchestras, but World War II intervened. He joined the Grenadier Guards and played in their orchestras. Humphrey Lyttleton, who was a Lieutenant in the Grenadier Gardens and saw action at Salerno tells a nice little story:

During my spell at the Guards Depot I began to brush up my trumpet-playing. Apart from the opportunity for practice provided by the long periods of inactivity, there were also quite a regular number of dances held in the main gymnasium. For these functions a unit from the regimental Band of the Grenadier Guards used to provide the dance music.

The standard was high, which is not surprising, because during the war many of the leading jazz and dance musicians were enlisted into the Household Brigade bands. So throughout the war many idols of the followers of popular music could be seen trudging along at the head of a column of guardsmen.

At one of the dances at Caterham I sat in on trumpet with the band. Being struck by the clarinet-playing of the bandsman sitting next to me I asked him what his name was. When he said: 'Nat Temple, sir,' I very nearly stood to attention and saluted."

When Nat was demobbed in 1944 he formed his own band, one of his earliest singers being a young Frankie Vaughan, who went on to be a star.

After some work with Butlin's holiday camps, he moved easily into radio and television, working with Bernard Braden and Barbara Kelly on *Breakfast with Braden*. His band also played on the radio show Music While You Work until 1983, and on the well-known TV show *Crackerjack*.

Of all the British-Jewish bandleaders save maybe Joe Loss, Nat worked with a massive number of A-list stars – such as Julie Andrews, Mel Torme, Hoagy Carmichael and Matt Monro. The reason was simple – he was an easy person to work with, and popular. It should not be forgotten that he also did Christmas parties at Windsor Castle for the Queen.

Incredibly, aged 82, he was nominated for an Emmy in New York for the music he composed for two poignant television programmes called *Igor, Child of Chernobyl* and *Igor, the Boy Who Dared to Dream*. He was also awarded the Freedom of the City of London.

He lasted the distance, only retiring from playing when he was 90, and died at his home in Woking, Surrey.

At his funeral in Randalls Park, Leatherhead it was said: "Such was his modesty and passion for playing in front of an audience, that he didn't actually care where he was working - whether it was for our royal family at royal palaces and castles, or at vast conferences all over Europe. He was equally at home playing in scout huts, golf clubs, pubs or synagogue halls. Nat loved them all."

Joe Loss OBE

Born in 1909 in Bishopsgate, Joshua Alexander Loss was almost the longest lasting bandleader of all, and certainly one of the best known – Jewish or non-Jewish.

The son of an immigrant (of course!), he learned to play the violin and we are told he was good enough to win a scholarship to the London School of Music. He was still a teenager when he formed his first band, playing at cinemas and dance halls - wherever he could find work. He also played at local cinemas, where he would accompany the silent movies of the day.

He formed his band in 1930 after learning his trade with other orchestras, and his career immediately moved up a gear. His band played at the Waldorf Astoria ballroom, one of the prime locations in London (a replica of this ballroom featured in the movie *Titanic),* and a couple of years later he was booked at the prestigious KitKat Club. He was then asked to make radio broadcasts, and Vera Lynn made her first broadcast with his orchestra in 1938. It was her first big break. He toured extensively with ENSA during the war years, and there is a nice photograph of him with Glen Miller and Vera Lynn.

Courtesy Jewish Museum

His band never lost its popularity, and for good reason. He would play any form of music as long as it was popular, and so his band never became out of date.

Julien Vedey said: "The first lesson (for musicians who played) with Joe Loss was to subjugate their individual music tastes to the requirements of the audience. The customer was always right." This was the exact opposite of what some other bandleaders did, but Loss backed his own judgement and was invariably correct.

As to his inner thoughts he once said that "the better the restaurant or hotel the lower the standard of dancing", adding "fortunately there are still thousands of young workers who take a pride in their dancing, and my band is their band - the band for dancers".

He played jazz/swing when it was appropriate, and he would play blues, or dance, or light classical or pop. When the dance halls started being pulled down, he moved into TV work, notably in the first iteration of *Come Dancing*.

A brief glance at one of his LPs from 1967 shows how he had adapted:

Joe Loss & His Orchestra – Top Pop Dance Time 1967:

Quickstep Medley: I'm A Believer, Georgy Girl Slow

Foxtrot Medley: Let's Go To San Francisco

Quickstep Medley: Thoroughly Modern Millie.

Slow Foxtrot Medley: A Whiter Shade Of Pale.

Beat Medley: Itchycoo Park / Ha! Ha! Said The Clown

The mind boggles at the thought of a dance band playing Itchycoo Park.

He was popular throughout the land and at the highest level – two days before Princess Margaret's wedding, the Queen gave a party for 2000 at Buckingham Palace in honour of the new couple, and it was no surprise that the Joe Loss Orchestra was the main band.

He was on *This is Your Life* twice, was awarded the OBE, and eventually retired some 50 years after his first band played at the Hammersmith Palais. Perhaps the greatest honour was that after he retired, the band played on with his name attached to it.

Oscar Rabin

Oscar Rabin was one of the best-known bandleaders in the land, although he was somewhat of a reluctant front man.

He was born Oscar Rabinowitz in Riga, Latvia in 1899, the son of a cobbler. The family moved to the East End and Rabin attended the Jewish Free School. He took up the violin and won a scholarship to the Guildhall School of Music in London.

Old enough to serve in the infantry in the First World War, he formed a band after the war and played at Lyons Corner House in the West End, probably Coventry Street. These Corner Houses had a great appeal to the middle classes (and should not be confused with the Tea Rooms). There was live music and within each Corner House there were several restaurants, each with their own band. Coventry Street Corner House seated 2,000 diners on multiple floors. It was the largest restaurant in the world, and therefore a great gig for an up and coming band to get. It enabled Rabin to become well known.

A Lyons Corner House Restaurant in the 1930s. Note the band on the right.

He first came to greater public notice in the 1920s leading a band called the Romany Five, and in the latter part of the decade he formed a partnership with a singer/actor/banjo player called Harry Davis, who would be the front man for what came to be called the Oscar Rabin Band.

The 1930s were the height of their success with long residencies at the Hammersmith Palais and the Astoria, Charing Cross Road, as well as many recordings.

Rabin was more of a manager than a bandleader, owning the Wimbledon Palais de Danse (which sadly ended its days as Furnitureland) and he preferred playing in the band as a saxophonist to leading it. Davis was the public face of the band, and this worked really well, with the partnership lasting 25 years. The band used his name and was highly successful, recording and touring the country, even during the war years, where his band also gave many ENSA concerts to entertain the troops.

In 1951 the partnership broke up, but Rabin carried on, notably having a five-year residency at Mecca's Lyceum Ballroom in the West End of London, consisting of a punishing schedule of six afternoon and six evening performances a week. It is noticeable that Melody Maker, the popular music magazine, rated Oscar's band in the top 10 most popular bands, even in the fifties.

One of his singers was the infamous comedian Bernard Manning.

Oscar died in Putney in 1958. His family carried on in the music business, notably Bernard, his son, who ran the Wimbledon Palais as a pop venue, hosting such as the Beatles, Rolling Stones, Pink Floyd, The Who and The Kinks.

Chapter 4 - Changing tracks

World War II had a different effect on some of those involved with the Golden Age. It gave them time to re-evaluate what they wished to do with their lives in the music business, and three people certainly took advantage of the interregnum. Interestingly enough, they had all worked for or with Bert Ambrose and Harry Roy.

Two of them were brothers, Sid and Woolf Phillips, whose careers took highly divergent paths, and the third, Stanley Black, who became one of the most respected figures in British light entertainment.

Sid Phillips

Isador Simon Phillips was one of those interesting characters active in the 1930s, who made the transition from the dance bands of the 1930s to the jazz of the 1950s. He was never a superstar, and is now largely forgotten, but he was massively influential, both pre-war and certainly post-war.

He was born in Mile End in 1907, beginning his musical career in a small band with his brothers Harry, Roy, and Woolf, successfully recording and touring. He wrote a massive amount of arrangements for Bert Ambrose, and, because of his skill with the clarinet, joined the orchestra in 1933, where he stayed until 1937.

World War II intervened and as a fluent linguist he became involved with intelligence work for the London Police and the RAF. After the war he formed a band of his own, the Dixieland Jazz Band, reputedly a favourite band of Princess Margaret, playing at Windsor Castle on occasion – and carried on recording.

His influence on the growing jazz scene in Britain was such that upcoming talents such as Kenny Ball found their feet with him. He continued playing and recording clarinet until his death in 1973 in Chertsey, Surrey.

Woolf Phillips

In Phillips' obituary in *the Guardian*, Michael Freedland noted: "Almost all of the big bandleaders who featured on 1940s BBC radio in its most influential and popular era were the sons of Jewish immigrants, and from London's East End. While their parents had wanted them to play the violin or piano, the sons found they could make more money fronting orchestras."

Rather unfairly, Freedland states that most of these were not musicians but, with the exception of Joe Loss, "just looked good in white tie and tails, waving a stick", which to my mind is just a cheap shot.

He is correct about the background, however.

He says: "Woolf Phillips stands out as the leader of the pack".

Phillips followed a well-worn track. At the beginning of his career he became well-known as one of the leading trombonists in the UK, and arranged for Ambrose and Harry Roy. Before World War II he was playing in various bands and composing and arranging for bandleaders such as Joe Loss, Ambrose and Harry Roy.

So far, so normal. What makes him stand out is his post-war career, when for six years he was musical director at the London Palladium at a time when it was at its peak of popularity. In that time, he performed with such as Frank Sinatra, Judy Garland, and Sammy Davis Jr.

When the hypocritical and quite racist Musicians' Union blocked entry to the UK for American bands, the promoter and manager Val Parnell sneaked Benny Goodman, one of the gods of jazz, in to play at the Palladium in 1949 by describing him as a "visiting artist" or "vaudeville acts" (Parnell's words). Goodman was not able to use his own sidemen, but rather used Woolf Phillips and his orchestra (called the Skyrockets). Some vaudeville act, and it must have been a wonderful opportunity for Woolf.

Furthermore, in 1950, when Frank Sinatra went on tour in the UK, it was with music arranged by Phillips that he did so. He is supposed to have described him as the finest conductor with whom he had ever worked.

Phillips moved into TV work, composing the theme tune for the popular TV show *What's My Line,* and in 1966 moved to California at the urging of his friend, Donald O'Connor (star of *Singing in the Rain*), where he became a notable and respected arranger, composer and conductor until his death in 2003.

The number of famous artists he worked with is too long for this book, but here is a small sample: Anthony Newly, Milton Berle, the Marx Brothers, Laurel and Hardy, Bob Hope, Jack Benny, Danny Kaye, Ella Fitzgerald, Maurice Chevalier, Noel Coward, Nat King Cole and George Formby.

Stanley Black OBE

There are three people who have a large obituary in the Jewish Chronicle – Nat Temple, Joe Loss….and Stanley Black.

Stanley Black (never Stan) grew up in the same environment as all the others, but his life took a divergent route. He moved from classical to dance music to light entertainment and became one of the most influential figures in British music. He broke the mould.

Born in Whitechapel in 1913 as Solomon Schwarz to Romanian parents, his mother from a rabbinic family, he began by studying piano and composition at the renowned Matthay School of Music, and his first classical composition was performed by the BBC Orchestra when he was 12.

He went almost straightaway into the London dance bands playing piano, which gave him an easy entrée into London dance bands as a pianist and arranger. Between 1933-1940 he played with Winnick, Stone, Roy, and Ambrose, to name but a few.

He had a peculiar talent. He could listen to a record and set down on paper every note played by each instrument so that another band could play the same score as the original; can you imagine how any bandleader would not walk over hot coals to have someone in his band with this talent?

When World War II began, he joined up, joining the RAF Band, but was invalided out on health grounds. Initially he went back to Harry Roy, but from then onwards what had been an unremarkable career took off. He went freelance and took up the baton, something he probably should have done 10 years earlier. He became leader of the BBC Dance Orchestra, from 1944-1951, also being the house conductor for Decca Records Company, for whom he produced up to four LPs a year.

He then had a glittering career playing a variety of music. He said: "Serious music needn't be pompous. *West Side Story* should be in the same programme as Beethoven". He became a man admired in the music world, conducting several symphony orchestras and writing music for films such as *The Long and the Short and the Tall* and the incidental music for *The Goon Show.*

He recorded many albums with his orchestra, and his breadth of talent was such that not only was he involved with 'serious' music but that he was willing to engage with the 'pop' genre. He composed the music for the films *Summer Holiday* (for which he won the Ivor Novello award in 1963 for the Year's Outstanding Score of a Musical) and *The Young Ones*. He guest-conducted all around the world, notably the Seoul Philharmonic Orchestra at the 1988 Olympics, and with the Boston Pops, and was finally awarded the OBE in 1986.

He didn't follow trends. He created them.

Chapter 5 - Minor Bandleaders

These were not in the same league as the Big Four, but they were highly talented and very popular.

Sydney Kyte was one – we have very few details for him other than that he led a band for 10 years at the Piccadilly Hotel in London until the war, and then vanished from the scene. Willie Stephany was another – a journeyman bandleader. A third was Felix King (Kaiser) who was based around clubs in London and had a successful radio career.

Others had a higher profile with interesting facets to their careers.

Benny Freedman

Benny came from the usual background of being born in the East End and playing for silent films, then having his own orchestra, playing at the Lyons Corner Houses like many.

Highly talented and well regarded, he was resident, according to his daughter, at Leas Cliff Hall, Folkestone and then came to Portsmouth in 1948, playing in the 1950s up to the mid-1960s at the Savoy Ballroom, Southsea.

He became "an institution at the Savoy Ballroom. On Friday nights, Benny and the boys would warm up the dancers before handing over the stage to the big-name guest outfits". He was a follower of strict tempo - Portsmouth News call him the "King of the Quick Quick Slow Brigade" in his obituary.

Finally, the diminishing interest in his type of music overtook him and he retired to teach at Portsmouth Grammar. He had never become one of the leading bandleaders, but on the other hand can be said to represent the many minor, but nonetheless highly regarded and talented bandleaders who plied their trade in the dance halls.

Benny Daniels

By the time Benny became a bandleader, the Golden Age was in its last death throes, but his career was an interesting one.

He was born in Hull around the turn of the century but is notable for not having been grown up in either the East End of London or the North West! He was born in Hull. At some point he left to live in London, because by 1935 he was in Jack Hylton's Dance Band, playing in Berlin.

In 1937 the band toured Germany again. Peter Faint in his biography of Jack Hylton takes up the story: " On January 11 , 1937, the band embarked on another European tour, travelling through Berlin, Prague and Vienna before settling into the Scala Theatre in Berlin for a month long run. … Nazi authorities were responsible for making sure there were no Jews visible in the band.

They spoke directly to Hylton about this and were assured that no performers of Semitic appearance were to be clearly on display at the front of the stage during the performance. Questions were asked about specific performers and Hylton deflected the questions and the band remained intact."

The specific performers in question were Benny, who was a saxophonist and Freddie Schweitzer, Clarinettist. Whether or not they went on tour with Hylton is not documented. It is probable, given Hylton's personality that they took who they wanted and hid them as best as they could.

When war came, Benny joined up and became a member of the Army's dance band, the Blue Sky Rockets, which he led after the war. The band disbanded in the 1950s, and the last we hear of him is as a bandleader with a residency at the Locarno Ballroom, Glasgow…and that is where we leave him. The last we know of him is in this item from the Radio Times in 1961

Peter West introduces the third heat in the nation-wide amateur ballroom dancing contest between twelve regions for the BBC Television Award and Formation Team Cup.

West Scotland
From The Locarno Ballroom, Glasgow **with Benny Daniels and his Orchestra.**
Compere, Alex Macintosh
v.

Benny Loban

Benny's star shone very briefly, but significantly.

He was born in the Ukraine in 1902, but the family emigrated to
Canada in 1913. It seems Benny was some sort of a talent for at 18
he won a scholarship to the Royal Academy of Music in London.
After his studies he returned to Canada, but in 1929, out of work,
returned to London

He was soon leading small ensembles at various Lyons Corner
Houses and then featured as violinist in the Savoy Orpheans, a
well-known band. He led the Orpheans on tour, starting in 1930,
and I guess for copyright reasons later changing its name to Bennie
(sic) Loban and His Music Weavers'.

He toured the UK from Birmingham to Plymouth, Glasgow to
Exeter. Here is a list of his engagements between 1933 and 1937,
showing the gypsy life that a conductor needed to have – but then
he was in his early thirties, and full of energy.

Feb 1933 - - Birmingham - West End Dance Hall
Aug 1933 - - Birmingham - West End Dance Hall
May 1934 - - Dundee - Broadway theatre
Jun 1934 - - Ayr, Scotland
Nov 1934 - - Birmingham - Hippodrome
Jun 1935 - - Chelsea - Garden Palace
Dec 1935 - - Exeter - Rougemont
Mar 1936 - - Leeds
Jun 1936 - - Lewisham - Hippodrome
Feb 1937 - - Glasgow - Alhambra Theatre
Jun 1937 - - Yarmouth - Britannia Pier

Radio Times, 10 February 1933,

It must have been a relief, though when in 1938, he was offered the opportunity to be the resident band at the Royal Bath Hotel in Bournemouth, and now he was being heard over the radio. He must have felt settled, but the war came.

The South Coast was not a safe place to be – there was one raid in 1943 that damaged over 3,300 buildings and killed many, and what is more, the Royal Canadian Air force took over the hotel, so it was time to move once more. For the whole war he headed the band at the prestigious Palais Ballroom in Glasgow, and made regular radio appearances.

However, as for many, World War 2 was the end of things, or to paraphrase Winston Churchill, the beginning of the end.

Benny returned to Canada in 1952, and spent the rest of his life in Real Estate, giving up the music business.

It is significant that many bandleaders changed career after World War 2 as they moved into middle age.

Albert McCarthy states "An article in a 1936 Radio Review detailed a week in Lew Stone's career at the time, the most striking fact being that on no single day did he sleep for longer than seven hours; working days of sixteen to eighteen hours were not uncommon.

Success on those terms was indeed hard earned, and, indeed, activity on such a scale was not uncommon for bandleaders during their peak years. Its effect on their health scarcely needs to be underlined. "

When the rewards diminished, many looked round for other options such as management, or even an end to involvement in the music business.

In Loban's case he had spent his career going from pillar to post, and it must have been a strain, not only on his family life, but on him physically, and I suppose he had had enough. He died in 1993.

Bert Firman

Those who study Jewish bandleaders will soon come across Ambrose, Joe Loss, Harry Roy, and Geraldo. Bert Firman, on the other hand, is one of those lesser-known mortals, who made an amazing contribution during his career, but then gave it all up, and vanished into obscurity.

He:

- Was probably once the youngest professional bandleader in the world, having begun at 16
- Was the first British musician to record George Gershwin's *Rhapsody in Blue*, playing it in 1928 soon after it was released in 1924
- Played with such giants as Django Reinhardt and Stéphane Grappelli
- Played for the future Edward VIII, while he was still the Prince of Wales, at his private parties

But he then gave it all up.

Herbert Feuerman was born in London in 1906, and his obituary tells an interesting story. Stereotypically, and with some truth, most Jewish parents want their child to become a lawyer or doctor, and not a musician (what sort of career is that?). Herbert wanted to become a doctor, but his family would have none of it: "Since his brothers, cousins, uncles and indeed father were musicians, he would be one too. Hence, Bert took up the violin."

Through his family's contacts he was soon playing in orchestras. Herbert Feuerman morphed into Bert Firman, and when the leader of the Metropole Hotel's Midnight Follies Orchestra became drunk and fell off the stage (!), he took over as bandleader.

By the age of 22 he was making records with his own band – 750 recordings with Zonophone alone – and in 1928 we have Bert Firman's Dance Orchestra playing only the eighth recording of *Rhapsody in Blue*.

He played at a number of locations, in those years, but it seems that he had wanderlust. He was also clearly the most metropolitan of all our bandleaders. He moved in 1929 to New York, conducting the NBC orchestra, then to Hollywood, working with Warner Brothers.

No sooner back in London, than off he went with a new band to Les Ambassadeurs in Paris. It seems that for a number of years he then alternated between Paris in the winter and Monte Carlo and Cannes in the summer, what he called "the usual lovely round of engagements that made that country a bandleader's paradise in those days", finally settling in London in 1937.

At the outbreak of World War II, he joined up and toured the Middle East, entertaining the troops. After the war it seems that he had doubts as to his future. In an interview for *Melody Maker* in 1945, he said: "Sydney Lipton and I were talking about the future only recently and we were wondering if we would be 'forgotten men' of this business when we came out of khaki."

He went to Paris and formed a band at the Bagatelle Club in Paris which featured Stéphane Grappelli and Django Reinhardt, but he knew his time had come and that the era of British dance bands was up. Only the strong would survive, and he never really had a base.

It seems, too, that he had fallen in love with a lady called Beatrice (to whom he would remain married for 50 years). Seamlessly, at the age of around 40 he left the music business and went to work as a broker for the London Metal Exchange, where he remained for the next 26 years until retirement. As his biography states "He still enjoyed meeting up with his old mates in the business until his death in 1999."

Sydney Lipton

Sydney Lipton, Bert Firman's mate, was another of those bandleaders born in London who did his apprenticeship with other bands.

Like Ambrose, his instrument of choice was the violin, playing in the Billy Cotton Orchestra, and recording with Ambrose, until finally he formed his own band in 1931. He took up residency at the Grosvenor Hotel in Westminster where he worked for an amazing 36 years (with a break for the war where he served in the Royal Artillery and Signals) – a quite extraordinary length of time.

Grosvenor House Ballroom 1933

A criticism of his brand of dance music was that it was anodyne and popularist; although fans called it sophisticated, smooth and polished! In his world, his audiences went to dance, not necessarily to listen.

He ended his days in California, moving there in 1967 to be with his daughter.

Harry Leader

He never reached the very top of the pile, and his career was not particularly exceptional, but many articles about those days mention him amongst Stone, Ambrose and the leading bandleaders of the time. His claim to fame was that he 'discovered' the singer Matt Monroe. And there can't be many (or even any) bandleaders who had a bus named after them.

Not a lot is known about Leader's personal life other than that he was twice married. Of some note is that his son Michael became moderately famous throughout Britain when he played the milkman in *EastEnders*, the well-known soap drama on TV.

Harry Leader was yet another of the East End boys, having been born in Poplar in 1906 as George Henry Lebys (probably Levi) and was the son of a musician, who, it is said, had been a Professor of Music in St Petersburg.

In a pattern we've seen before, he self-taught himself a musical instrument - the saxophone this time. Being the son of a professional musician turned grocer must have helped. He also followed the regular pattern amongst his bandleading contemporaries by playing at the silent movies.

Having gained experience, he then played sax for a variety of bands, notably that of Sid Phillips and his Melodians in 1928. He started his own band, but his main focus seems to have been in the studio, churning out hit after hit, notably *Little Man. You've had a Busy Day.*

As a bandleader, there was quite a lot of hostility towards him. In 1950 Vedey noted in his book that: "No other bandleader has subjugated his own personal taste in dance music so completely to the requirement of the public as Harry Leader", which, given that the tone of his book is extreme sycophancy, is as close to criticism as one could get.

Leader did not get on well with other bandleaders, either; many blocked their musicians from recording with him, thus ensuring that he was never offered a long-term recording contract.

In 1939 he took up the baton more or less permanently, just at the end of the Golden Age, and when he did, it was not at one of the posh cafés, restaurants and hotels that others had played at. Instead Harry Leader's first residency was at the Hammersmith Palais from around 1939 to 1942, after which he moved to the Astoria until 1955.

Latterly he moved down to Brighton to be the resident at the Regent Ballroom, where he stayed until well into the sixties, and began composing tunes with his second wife and teaching.

Like Joe Loss, he was a survivor; he but I have the feeling that his happiest time was when he went to Brighton. Perhaps he was happier away from the bright lights, and the other Bandleaders.

He was so well regarded in the town that when Brighton and Hove were looking for someone to name one of their buses after, they used him (photo below shows Michael, his son, with the bus).

Sidney Simone

One of those journeymen conductors, who followed rather than led, Sidney Wexler was born in 1913, the son of, yes you guessed it, a tailor. He received formal training at the Royal College of Music, but then followed the well-worn path of accompanying silent films, before joining Geraldo in his Gaucho Tango Orchestra.

He became lead violin with Geraldo, but at some point he began conducting, and acquired minor recognition when he appeared at the Savoy Hotel, and later during World War II when he substituted for Bert Ambrose on ENSA tours.

By 1939 he had changed his surname to Simone, no doubt because Simone is a little smoother than the rather teutonic sounding Wexler.

**Simone with Noel Coward and Charlie Chaplin
(photo source unknown)**

Post-war he was very successful, his band accompanying the stars of the day such as Frankie Vaughan, Judy Garland and Diana Ross. I think it fair to say that his orchestra was obviously popular amongst the stars, and that speaks volumes about the quality of his work, and his organising and arranging ability.

He was noted for playing for royalty, notably the Duke and Duchess of Windsor at their home in the South of France, but also Prince Rainier of Monaco.

In latter years he ran a theatrical agency.

Chapter 6 - The Northern Set

North Manchester

Now here's a funny thing. During the Golden Age of Dance Bands, there were vast numbers of professional and semi-professional dance bands in and around Merseyside, but there are no historical records that any of the bandleaders were Jewish.

One assumes that plenty of the musicians were Jewish, and as demonstrated by Frankie Vaughan and Brian Epstein, Jews from the area were not averse to involving themselves in the music business. However, with the rare exception of Johnny Rosen, who was not from the area in any case, it was a Jewish bandleader desert.

It seems that Merseyside could provide Jewish singers, comedians, playwrights, but not a bandleader. It was Manchester in the North West that would provide bandleaders, and in particular, North Manchester.

In many ways it was the 'East End' of Manchester, for as with the East End in London, immigrants had come in and congregated around an area, and then moved upmarket. In this case the area they came to was called Strangeways, and when they found their feet, their move upmarket was to Cheetham Hill and the surrounding areas - Salford, Prestwich and Crumpsall.

There was a vibrant immigrant community in these areas; as in the rest of the country dance became big, and there were massive opportunities to be had for the children of immigrants who were looking for openings.

Some of the best known dance bandleaders of the 20th century came from the North West. Most never made it out of there – and when one considers that the Blackpool Tower Ballroom held 3,000, and that there was a plethora of ballrooms outside London to enable an ambitious musician to make a living, one can understand why they stayed.

North Mancunian bandleaders from Prestwich such as Mick Farber and Ralph Gethic were happy to ply their trade mostly around the North West pre- and post-war; and while Gethic also had a residency at the Grosvenor Hotel, Manchester, they were small fry compared to the Geraldos of the world of ballroom dancing.

In fact, they constantly faced competition from the major bandleaders, who were always willing to come North to earn extra cash. Who could possibly compete with Ambrose when he was able to bring Vera Lynn and Max Bacon on his appearances?

There was also Julian Leon Niman, born in Higher Broughton, Salford in 1893. He formed Julian Niman's Scarlet Syncopators, which made radio broadcasts, and became musical director of the short-lived Mancunian Films Corporation.

However, as with Farber and Gethic he never really left the North West, and like Farber his band was really no more than a bar mitzvah and wedding band - although it should be noted that Niman occasionally had high-profile gigs at the Mecca and Ritz dance halls. He died after the Second World War aged 59.

There were others.

Maurice Winnick

Someone who attended the same school as Niman was Maurice Winnick, who took a different path. Maurice was born in Salford in 1902, studied the violin at the Royal College of Music, Manchester, and, we are told, was briefly a vocalist for Niman. He progressed beyond his beginnings, for we are told that while still in his teens he led a band on a transatlantic liner.

In the book *Manchester's Music Makers*, Phil Moss tells us how Winnick played in local bands, becoming leader of his own orchestra in Manchester. His career then completely changed tack. He moved to Nottingham in 1928 to take over the band at the Palais, and by the 1930s he had moved to London where, as Moss says, his good fortune resembled that of a fairy story.

source unknown

He appeared at many of the major venues in London such as the Hammersmith Palais de Danse, made records, and performed on the radio. Finally, and this was the pinnacle of a career as a bandleader, he gained a residency at a leading London hotel, succeeding Harry Roy at the Dorchester.

His style was inoffensive, almost analgesic – his theme tune was *the sweetest music this side of heaven*, which tells you everything.

However, Winnick was nothing if not forward looking. After touring with his band entertaining the troops during World War II, he saw the writing on the wall and gave up bandleading, concentrating on being a successful booking agent, bringing over TV shows from the USA to Britain, such as *What's My Line*. He died in London in 1962, after a successful career.

Nat Bookbinder

Nat Bookbinder was in many ways unique. Not only was he a bandleader, but at the same time also a musical agent, and for a few years he was the owner of a ballroom/nightclub – and he stayed in and around the North West all his life.

Nathan Buchbinder was born in London on 13 April 1908, the son of immigrants from Eastern Europe. The family soon moved to Prestwich in (guess where) North Manchester, and aged 14, the young Nathan was set to work in the cotton mills. According to the Crewe Chronicle, pretty soon after that he took up music and left the mills far behind. At age 17, he could be found performing at the Queens Hotel, Piccadilly, and later the Café Royal, both in the centre of Manchester.

This would seem to be somewhat of a leap, from cotton mill to dance band, but it was not unusual for the children of immigrants to take up music, as witness London's East End. It was the same with Ambrose, Geraldo, Sid Phillips, and it must have been true of Nat. In his case it was the drums, and as there was a huge demand for musicians in the rapidly expanding world of the dance hall, it would have been relatively easy for him to get a job.

Somewhere between the late 1920s and the 1930s, Nat gave up the drumstick and took up the baton, but he also became an impresario and theatrical agent. We first meet him in the press when his name appears in a newspaper on 8 July 1936, which reads as follows: "Nat Bookbinders Musical Enterprises – offers Musicians and Bands (Graded men only). Quality of performance guaranteed." Prior to this he was managing director of 'British Bands and Cabarets Ltd', which was based in Queen Street, Blackpool.

NAT BOOKBINDER
and his Six Chapters will give a
programme of dance music from the
studio this evening at 6.15.

As such he would have had fingers in many pies and became very
well-known around the North West in the late 1930s; he had a
residency at the Café Royal, broadcast on the BBC Regional
Programme five times between February 1937 and March 1938,
and on one occasion his band, the Chapters, featured Al Bowlly,
one of the most famous singers in the UK. He certainly raked in
enough money for him to open a dance hall/night club called the
Casino Club in Warrington (between Manchester and Liverpool) in
December 1938.

He made no recordings that I know of, but it seems that the band
was capable of either straight 'old-time dance' or swing – the Club
had an old art deco feel, with photos of such as Duke Ellington and
Count Basie adorning the walls.

When the war came, Bookbinder made sure to offer discounted entry to the armed forces. Unsurprisingly, the music played in the club was swing, and by 1942 the Casino Club had become the place to go in Warrington. The US Armed Forces moved into the old RAF base near the town, and suddenly they were 'over here', and Bookbinder had to adapt to an influx of young, testosterone-driven men from another country, who might not appreciate the mores of a foreign land.

Initially this was not a problem. US personnel who had dates would go to pubs, then the cinema, and end up at the Casino Club "where the crowd would jitterbug the night away to the sound of Nat Bookbinder and his dance band".

Then it all changed. Came the day when a young man called Herbert Greaves turned up at the club. Herbert was Jamaican, and at the time the US Army was segregated, with blacks being treated as second-class citizens. As far as the American soldiers were concerned, the Casino Club was a whites-only establishment, and soldiers at the dance made that clear to Bookbinder.

He then received a letter which went like this: "It is not our intention to dictate the policies of privately-owned establishments, but in the interest of eliminating trouble in which our troops may be involved, we will appreciate your cooperation in prohibiting Negroes from attending the dances."

He was told that this was being done to "keep the peace", especially as a number of US forces personnel were from the Southern United States. If he didn't comply, his club would be out of bounds to all US personnel.

Bookbinder was having none of this. In *History Today* we are told that Nat said that he would "place the ballroom out of bounds to white Americans rather than forbid the attendance of coloured British subjects". For him, if you were fit to fight for the country, you were "fit to mix".

Amazingly, the British, no doubt driven by their own prejudices against blacks and Jews, and a desire to be compliant and servile to the American authorities, failed to back up Bookbinder, and banned all British military personnel! You couldn't make it up, could you, especially as this was seemingly the only place where a colour bar existed – in the bright lights of London, jazz clubs were unsegregated.

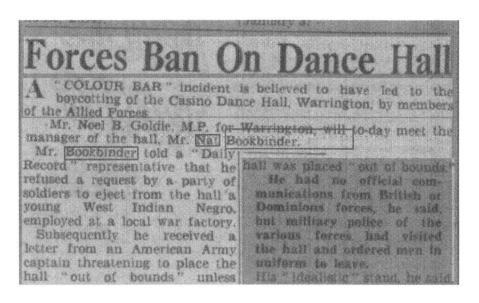

Forces Ban On Dance Hall

A "COLOUR BAR" incident is believed to have led to the boycotting of the Casino Dance Hall, Warrington, by members of the Allied Forces.

Mr. Noel B. Goldie, M.P. for Warrington, will to-day meet the manager of the hall, Mr. Nat Bookbinder.

Mr. Bookbinder told a "Daily Record" representative that he refused a request by a party of soldiers to eject from the hall a young West Indian Negro, employed at a local war factory.

Subsequently he received a letter from an American Army captain threatening to place the hall "out of bounds" unless hall was placed "out of bounds."

He had no official communications from British or Dominions forces, he said, but military police of the various forces had visited the hall and ordered men in uniform to leave.

His "idealistic" stand, he said,

Bookbinder had some support from the good people of Warrington, but no support from his MP, nor from the War Department in the form of Percy Grigg, the Secretary of State, who stated that the ban was because of the danger of overcrowding, which was clearly a lie. Grigg then confirmed the ban on British soldiers.

The embargo worked. The Casino Club was empty most nights, and the ban was strictly enforced. The Club closed soon afterwards. Bookbinder was a victim of out-and-out racism and indifference. He estimated it cost him £150,000 (ITM).

He never regained the momentum he had in the late 1930s. He made a living. We have him and his Tropical Rhythm Band in the late 1940s playing at the Blackley Palais in North Manchester, but he had a growing family, and one guesses that with the demise of dance bands, he needed to rethink. He retired from the business and opened a shop in North Manchester selling jewellery, and he had a jewellery stall on Crewe market - a long way from his life in music.

The Bookbinder family was very well known in North Manchester. His sons followed him into the music business, opening a club called Bookbinders in Manchester, and his niece, Ellen Bookbinder, gained fame as Elkie Brooks with the band Vinegar Joe.

Nat Bookbinder may have only been a bit player in the entertainment industry. However, at one time he was at the very core of the dance revolution in the North West, and made a stand that to this day ranks as one of the finest examples of the fight against racism. A mensch – a person of integrity and honour.

Johnny Rosen – The hard life

Of the Northern bandleaders, there was one who is now almost forgotten. His life can only be pieced together by clues here and there – the odd cutting from a newspaper, a death certificate, the occasional mention in a Google search.

He represents the myriad bandleaders who graced the ballrooms outside London during the 1930s and his story shows the hard life behind the glitz and the glamour. He never reached the heights of Ambrose, Geraldo, Loss, and the others. It could not be said that his work was influential. It is also a somewhat tragic story.

There is little known about John Henry Rosen's early life. He is likely to have been born in 1897 in Reading to one Israel Rosen who had been living in Shoreditch, and in the 1911 census he is shown as living in Whitechapel. No doubt his father went where the jobs were. The first time we are made aware of Rosen's existence as a musician is when he appears as a violinist in the famous Jack Hylton's band in the early 1920s, specifically as a soloist on some of Hylton's records.

Courtesy Roy Star: Jack Hylton and the Queens Dance Orchestra, with Nat Star just behind Hilton, and Johnny Rosen at the front on clarinet- 1922

Harry Francis in his essay *Jazz Development in Britain* states that "in those days a regular ingredient of the Hylton programme was a waltz, the finale of which always came with Rosen standing to play the last bars accompanied only by the piano, and with a blue spot concentrated on his fingerboard as all other lights were dimmed."

Hylton had a different philosophy to the other bandleaders – he was not interested in taking up a residency with a hotel or ballroom but preferred touring the country, and going abroad. The schedule was punishing – a typical tour would be six weeks, six days a week and performances twice a day. In 1928 he was offered £42,000 for a one-year contract at the newly rebuilt Leicester Square Theatre, which also had a ballroom. In today's money this is a gobsmacking £2.6 million.

He stated that he could earn more money touring and selling records, and Johnny Rosen was part of this, as this band list from Paris shows:

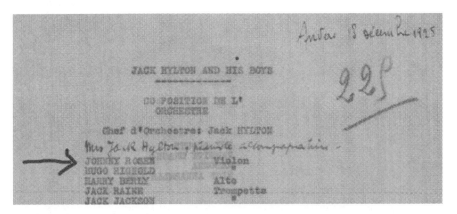

As said, it was punishing, and for any number of reasons Rosen must have decided that enough was enough, and that he needed to be his own master, for he split from Hylton in 1934, and attempted to form his own band in London, hoping to be attached to a hotel. He overreached himself. His band was too big and costly, and I can only guess that in the early 1930s there were plenty of bands that could undercut Rosen.

He found employ in Liverpool and Manchester at the Lewis's Department Store restaurant. This sounds odd until you realise that the Manchester store was well known for having a full-scale ballroom, and tea dances were a regular pastime in the more salubrious of restaurants and cafés.

On the top floor of the site was a ballroom with a sprung dancefloor, which was used for staff parties, next to a restaurant and cafeteria. In the Liverpool store the Tudor restaurant had a small area where shoppers could be serenaded.

When Rosen went to the North West, none of his London sidemen would follow him, nor seemingly his wife and two children, so he filled his band mainly with Liverpudlians. He would have found this easy to do. In the depression years of the 1930s there were many semi-professional bands, and many musicians for whom a place in Rosen's Orchestra and a steady wage was bliss.

By 1935 he seems to have broken up with his wife, and had a new famlly, settling in Wallasey, south of Liverpool. He was paying maintenance of around £15,000/year (in today's money), almost double the average national wage. With a new child in 1937, and a new partner, by 1937 he was supporting two families.

Nonetheless his band was fairly successful, and on top of his residency at Lewis's he took the band round the country – see Appendix 5. His earnings just from the Liverpool and Manchester Lewis's were, however, in the region of around £80-100,000 per year ITM.

Then it all went wrong. To begin with, Hitler invaded Poland! I alluded earlier to the fact that after war was declared people stopped going to dances in the same volume as before – many of the men who went dancing were now in the armed forces, and what with the blackout, life was suspended (à la coronavirus). Once the Liverpool Blitz began it was inevitable that his lucrative job with Lewis's should also disappear, and in May 1941 they terminated his contract.

He carried on with his band – there is an advert in the Lancashire Burnley Express on 11th March 1942 for Johnny Rosen and his band, but the opportunities must have been few and far between. In January 1943 he filed for bankruptcy. He was now living at another address in Wallasey. Using today's money (2020) for clarity, he owed:

Arrears of income tax: £20,500
Arrears of maintenance payments: £11,500
Arrears to moneylender: £5000
Liabilities: £41,000

Total: £78,000
Assets: £2000

It is this latter amount that gives pause for thought. After a high-earning career, his assets were meagre. This was all he was left with. It was probably his musical instruments.

In June 1943 he contracted pneumococcal meningitis, and died in Birkenhead Hospital. No more is heard of him or his family, except that he had a brother in North London and that he is buried in Rainham Cemetery in Essex, near his mother, who died six years later. He passes into history, almost unnoticed. A tragic end for someone who was at the core of British dance bands for 23 years.

Phil Moss and the end of the Line

Of those that came out of the North West, Phil Moss had the longest career, and perhaps, when you consider that Maurice Winnick's star only shone brightly for a short while, Moss was the most successful of the bandleaders from the North West.

There is a good argument to say he was the last of the great Jewish bandleaders.

Born in 1914 in Newton Heath, North Manchester, Moss's route to fame was somewhat unusual, for he came to it as a trumpet player via the bugle band of the Jewish Lads Brigade, and via brass bands. No Royal College of Music for him or playing at cinemas.

He progressed to playing in house bands at weddings and at dance venues – and all over the country. He even played in Harry Roy's band at least once. The war intervened and he joined the RAF, playing in its band. Once the war was over he auditioned for the Joe Loss band, which was in Manchester on one of its tours, and for the next three years he was part of the setup.

He decided to strike out on his own; he married in 1947, and it is probable he wanted a more settled life, so he left the Joe Loss band, returned to Manchester, and set up his own band. He still followed the Loss philosophy: whatever was popular was good enough.

In 1954, he was given the residency at the Ritz ballroom in Manchester, where he stayed for 17 years, was featured on radio and television, notably on the BBC show *Come Dancing*, and in 1969 his band was the only one outside London to win the Carl-Alan Award for being the top dance band in the UK.

Year on year he would follow the dancing public of Manchester on their holidays to Blackpool and the Isle of Man, always adapting to the current trends. What marked him from his mentor, Joe Loss, was that he saw himself as an entertainer first, and that the music was just part of the entertainment.

There was Bastille Night, where he dressed as Napoleon, with the band being clothed in 'typical' French clothing (berets, striped waistcoats and sunglasses, waving French flags etc) and where he announced all the tunes in pidgin French, Halloween Night (where the band wore sunglasses, vampire masks and the like), St Patrick's Night, St David's Night, Seaside Nights (with the band attired in casual holiday clothes) and so on.

He had his small moment of fame too. In the award-winning film 'A Taste of Honey' his band is shown briefly as a backdrop to the action taking place (below). However, it is a case of blink and you'll miss it.

The '50s and '60s were his best years, but he saw that the writing was on the wall as far as the future for live dance music was concerned. He wrote: "When the professional bands were shunted into the sidelines some still fought on, through optimism, self-belief, or just love of the business".

In his case, he went freelance to keep his options nimble, and so carried on until the '90s. When he finally retired, he wrote three books about the Manchester music scene. He died in Crumpsall, North Manchester, in 2007.

To restate, Phil Moss was the last of what could be called the great dance bandleaders of the 20th century. He retired soon after Joe Loss gave up the baton, and with the retirement of these two, an era came to an end.

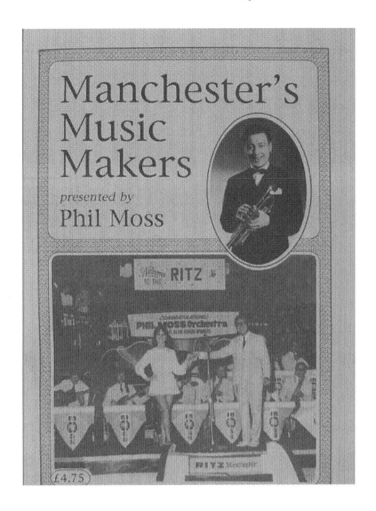

Chapter 7 - Yiddishkeit

Assimilation and Dissimulation

For the most part they had grown up in a Jewish community where they ate kosher, spoke Yiddish, wore tzitzis and had been barmitzvah'd.

Once they left the confines of the Jewish area, whether in London or Manchester, keeping the faith was going to be difficult. A sideman or bandleader's life was a seven day a week job.

If not touring, or broadcasting, they might be recording, and Saturday was no longer the holy day it might have been when they were growing up.

They were not in a Jewish environment any more. They needed to lose any trace of where they had come from and weren't being paid to play music from the 'Old Country'. Indeed, to their audience there was no 'Old Country'. Especially in London, they were playing to people who had distinct anti-Semitic proclivities.

So they needed to dissimulate – to wear a mask.

It was not a good idea to have a name such as Louis Steinberg, Harris Lipman, Herbert Feurmann, Nathan Buchbinder, Oscar Rabinowitz, or Solomon Schwarz given the underlying anti-Semitism and anti-foreigner feelings in the country, so they became Bert Ambrose, Harry Roy, Lew Stone, Syd Lipton, Stanley Black, Bert Firman, and Harry Leader.

They were Joe Loss rather than Joseph Loss, Nat Temple rather than Nathan, but obliquely instead of Gerald Bright there was Geraldo – which was however a Latin name and therefore sexy.

This dissimulation went further. Whether at the posh Café Anglais or the more proletarian Palais de Danse the punters weren't interested in hearing klezmer, and they most certainly did not want their bandleaders to have heavy regional accents.

At the posh places they wanted the bandleaders to be 'one of them', and at places like the Palais they wanted the bandleaders to be 'gents' - so the boys from the East End/London became 'proper' English gentlemen, glossy hair and all, with accents to match, and Joe Loss hid his tzitzis underneath his tuxedo. Even the Mancunian Winnick looked smooth as silk.

Londoners lost their accents (Geraldo was the exception); they wore no beards; they wore the correct gear; they not only dissimulated, they assimilated.

The arch assimilator was Harry Roy. His first marriage to Elizabeth Brooke was not only a match maybe of love, but also a statement. Given his background the match was very surprising, but he was a good-looking man, full of personality, and wealthy with it, and she was beautiful, and also dynamic.

However, at no point in his life do we hear of him playing a Hebrew tune, and while he was a glutton for publicity, there is no record of him supporting Jewish charities.

For Jews though, there is no escape. In a court case in 1933, where there was dispute over a hotel bill it was recorded that Roy, when he correctly refused to pay a bill was called a "dirty Jew". As his co-religionists in Germany were finding out, all the assimilation in the world meant nothing at the end of the day.

Struck By Handbag.

Defendant said when he came out of the hotel he saw the woman arguing and he asked her what was the matter. She explained the matter of booking rooms and when his brother offered her £1 for her trouble she declared that she wanted twelve guineas. Seeing the woman's attitude he advised his brother not to give her anything and she called him a "dirty Jew" and struck him in the face with her handbag. Witness put out his hand to ward off the blow and caught her in the face. He had been in the musical profession for forty years and had never had a previous experience of such a nature. After the incident the woman went up the steps

There were those, though, that largely kept to the faith as best they could, of whom Joe Loss was one – perhaps at the other end of the spectrum from Roy.

Loss kept his links with his roots. He was married in the full light of publicity at the Central Synagogue, London, and according to his daughter wore a tallis katan (tzitzis), underneath his tuxedo at dances.

He told stories about his time in Birmingham in the war and his search for matzo during Pesach, and how he avoided working on Rosh Hashanah, the Jewish New Year.

Jew-ish

When I began researching this book, I made a false assumption. That because none of them were mad religious, they had

completely lost all contact with their roots. They were Jews only in
the sense of Jonathan Miller's "Jew-ish" (according to the Jewish
Chronicle, Miller once said "I'm not really a Jew. Just Jew-ish. Not
the whole hog, you know"). The use of the word hog is unfortunate,
though.

As I dug deeper for information, a richer tapestry of observance
evolved. Some had been members of synagogues, some had been
involved in Jewish organisations, some were buried in Jewish
cemeteries.

I began with obituaries, and with memorial services, and I found that
a number many had a Jewish burial or cremation service, thus:

Joe Loss – Bushey Lane
Bert Ambrose – Bushey Lane
Geraldo – Willesden Jewish Cemetery
Oscar Rabin – Willesden Jewish Cemetery
Maurice Winnick – Hoop Lane Jewish Cemetery
Johnny Rosen – Rainham Jewish Cemetery
Nat Temple – Randalls Park Crematorium South London Liberal
Sid Phillips – Golders Green Crematorium
Stanley Black Edgewarebury Jewish Cemetery
Charles 'Nat' Star (Appendix 1) – East Ham Orthodox Cemetery

Of the others there is no trace, except that Harry Roy was cremated
at Golders Green. No doubt his family had a part to play in that. His
second wife Sonia Roy outlived him, and I believe would have taken
direction from them. Sid Phillips too at Golders Green Crematorium.

Research show also that Winnick was a member of West End
Synagogue, Rabin of Clapton Synagogue, and Nat Star Chingford
and Highams Park Synagogue.

Nat Star is maybe typical. He showed very little sign in his career of
being Jewish, but registered with a synagogue. His wife, according
to their grandson, Roy Star, continued to go on high holydays.

There was that little spark.

Then there were the surprises. The Jewish Chronicle "In Memoriam" pages told us that that Woolf Phillips was Life President of East Ham and Manor Park Synagogue, having served on their committee for many years, and in 1931 Gerald Bright put this notice in the Jewish Chronicle.

BRIGHT –Mr. Gerald Bright wishes his
'relatives and many friends, including
the St. Anne's Hebrew Congregation,
a very happy and prosperous New
Year and well over the Fast –3s. The
Avenue, Brondesbury Park, N.W.6

Clearly, in his time in St Anne's, Geraldo had made many friends. The notice appeared the following year as well. Of course it is possible that his mother put it in, as mothers do.

The Bookbinders were a well-known Mancunian Jewish family, and certainly supported Jewish charities. As a sign of his prominence in the music scene, Nat Bookbinder was able to get Gracie Fields to sing in Warrington for him in aid of the Manchester Jewish Soup Kitchen, and he was a member of the Association of Jewish Ex-Servicemen (AJEX).

Nat Temple's obituary mentions his support for Jewish causes, and Stanley Black's obituary tells of how he supported the Ravenswood (now Norwood Ravenswood) charity for young people with learning disabilities, on one occasion conducting at a concert at the Barbican for the charity's 40th anniversary. He was also Life President of the Celebrities Guild, a Jewish charity.

Lew Stone was an enigma. Biographies do not expose the inner man, and how he felt about Judaism. He may have married into the white Christian Shire upper middle-class fraternity, but his wife, Joyce, didn't conform to the stereotype.

That he should be so bold as to record and play a Yiddish song speaks volumes about how he felt about his heritage. Clearly he was a massive supporter of Israel, and after his death and his widow supported WIZO and even endowed a concert hall in a kibbutz in his name.

Jewish Music

After the Golden Age came Jewish jazz-band leaders, such as Monty Sunshine and Johnny Franks.

Franks is an interesting character, for he recorded Yiddish songs at a time when they were totally out of vogue; when few people in the world, let alone Britain, were recording them.

His band was known as the Johnny Franks Quartet, but when he was recording Yiddish songs he changed it to Johnny Franks and his Kosher Ragtimers. He made at least two Yiddish songs, *Mazel* and *Wilhemina* in 1951, and to be frank (sic) they were the type of songs played in Manhattan in 1915. He was 40 years behind his time, but Franks will have guessed that there was still a market in the Jewish community for this type of song and that it would go down a treat. He was right. It did. He was in high demand for years.

It is worth mentioning him because he wore his Judaism on his sleeve, the complete opposite to the Jewish bandleaders in this book, who, for the reasons I have already mentioned, avoided playing 'Kosher', unless they were at a Jewish function, e.g. a charity do or simcha, such as a wedding or bar mitzvah.

It was Lew Stone, who had in fact married out of his religion, who was left to be the only bandleader to record a Yiddish tune during the Golden Age. He recorded a song of such quality and passion that one feels that his heart was still with his roots, notwithstanding his success.

The song was called *A brivele der Mamen* (A Letter to Mama), and was by Solomon Smulewitz. Al Bowlly sang it in its original Yiddish. Without the lyrics a non-Jewish audience would have seen it as just another nice tune, but Stone (unlike non-Jewish bandleader, Ray Noble), at the suggestion of Lew Davis, his trombonist, recorded it in Yiddish. Both Stone and Davis, as the sons of immigrants will have understood the meaning – a man writing a letter to his mother, knowing he will never see her again. It has been described as one of the schmaltziest tissue-soaking tearjerkers in the repertoire of sentimental American Yiddish popular song.

Bowlly, of Greek and Lebanese extraction, was not Jewish, but he was taught the Yiddish intonation at Stone's home, and wrung every drop of emotion out of the song. When it was introduced, in 1933, it "stopped the show" at the London Palladium. It is the only example of a bandleader of the 20s or 30s playing a Yiddish song. By the way, *Bei Mir Bist du Schon* doesn't count as it is an Americanisation of the original.

Stone also made some records with Leo Fuld, the doyen of Yiddish song, in 1947 and 1948.

Nat Temple played at Jewish weddings, and so did Phil Moss. Probably bar mitzvahs too.

We come to Ambrose, inevitably. It was quite normal for a bandleader to record or play novelty tunes (quite often I guess to give a break from the dancing) in the finest spirit of music hall. In Ambrose's case there was a ditty called *Cohen the Crooner,* sung by his drummer, Max Bacon, about a market stall holder in Petticoat Lane in the East End. Bacon (himself Jewish) sang it in a mittel European accent.

Nowadays we tend to refer to this confirmation of stereotyping as Jewface, and it is highly frowned upon - the grasping Jew, not quite 'one of us', and with titles such as *Cohen Owes Me 97 Dollars, When Mose With His Nose Leads The Band.* Most of these were written by Jews for Jews specifically for the New York market. In those days, it was seen as just a bit of fun (by non-Jews, of course), but although the humour was gentle, it reinforced the stereotype of Jews as traders and outsiders.

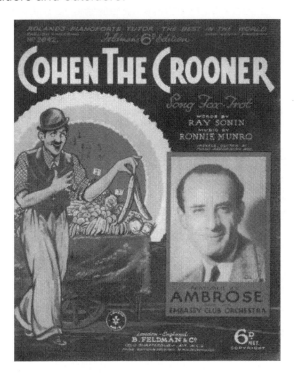

Much worse in many ways is the song *Izzy Azzy Wozz?* performed by the Jack Hylton Orchestra. The original lyrics are to be found in Appendix 3. This is a 'Jewish comedy foxtrot' dating back to 1929. Its origin is unclear, possibly written by Arthur Leclerq and recorded by Randolph Sutton, and also possibly by Irving Caesar of Tin Pan Alley.

The recording by Sutton is very straightforward and the diction, in very posh English, tells of a Jewish lawyer who is concerned about his client Izzy Rosenberg who is ill. Just to make sure you understand that Izzy is Jewish, a separate recording by Percival

McKay intersperses a couple of bars of *Khosn Kale Mazeltov* with the tune.

As with *Cohen Owes Me 97 Dollars*, the lawyer stereotypically is only really concerned about Izzy because Izzy owes him money. Jack Hylton recorded the number, and the vocal duo he used gave the lawyer a 'Jewish accent' mispronouncing bronchitis (as a foreigner would do) and stating that Izzy fell ill because he ate too many bagels, kishke, and lokshen. He also intermingles the music with a couple of bars from *Hatikvah* (and randomly, *Rhapsody in Blue*).

The vocal duo was the seemingly very non-Jewish Max and Harry Nesbitt (Darren) whose real surnames were Horowitz (!). I suspect Hylton gave them free reign, and they went back to their origins to add verses about kishkes, lokshen, and bagels, as well as to create the comic accent. Thankfully this tune has now disappeared into the mists of time.

As an aside, Harry's son, Derren, was the archetypal Gestapo Aryan Nazi in *Where Eagles Dare*. Oy!

Coming back to Cohen the Crooner, was it OK for Ambrose, a Jew, to perform this stereotypical number? It was almost as though Ambrose himself was distancing himself, and certainly there is no evidence that he had any links with the Jewish community (except for the fact he is buried in a Jewish cemetery!).

In fact, unlike Bookbinder, his views on race were probably quite in line with those of the day, for there are a couple of records that he made where the N-word was used. It is likely that he, like Harry Roy, considered himself assimilated. Like Roy, though he never had a problem including black musicians in his bands.

He produced a tune called *A Selection of Hebrew Dances* – a sort of mishmash of various tunes, but it was arranged by Sid Phillips,

who had a little more Yiddishkeit. In many ways it showed
Ambrose's limitations.

On the reverse side of the coin, Stanley Black was outstanding in
his understanding and love for Jewish music. Black had come from
the East End, as had Ambrose, but his Judaism was stronger – for
example his marriage (to Edna Kerber, a singer) in 1947 took place
in St John's Wood Synagogue.

He also clearly kept in touch with the culture for in 1965 he
produced, (with the London Festival Chorus & London Festival
Orchestra), two albums, showing that he hadn't left his heritage
behind. They were called *Spirit of a People* and *Music of a People*,
with a diverse set of offerings such as the theme from *Exodus,
Freilach, My Yiddishe Momma*, and *Kol Nidre*.

Another album *Mazel Tov! – Jewish Wedding Favourites* credits
Stanley Black and His Orchestra on one side and Sol Schwartz (get
it?) and His Orchestra on the other. He conducted the *Spirit* music
at the Royal Albert Hall in 1968 to celebrate Israel's 50th
anniversary.

Summary

After the East End, North Manchester and elsewhere they all went
their own way, musically and religiously.

Some, like Harry Roy left their religion altogether, others like
Stanley Black, Woolf Phillips and Joe Loss hung on to it. Religion
did not play a big part in their lives, but a number showed that they
recalled their roots, as did Lew Stone.

I also like to think that on occasions when they met at a social level
some reminiscences of the old days took place, and just a little bit of
Yiddish was spoken.

Chapter 8 - The phone stops ringing

Some of the bandleaders just carried on until they passed away. They never returned to the heights of their profession, but as with Sid Phillips just warbled away until their health ran out, or like Nat Temple carried on and then retired in their old age.

Some had changed tracks altogether, such as Woolf Phillips and Stanley Black, but when the producers of *Strictly Come Dancing* needed a dance orchestra of the highest quality, they had to rely on session musicians. There were no major bands left that they could call on.

Phil Moss told the story:

"One by one, my contemporaries were disappearing from the scene. The number of band engagements was dwindling ominously. The phone was silent for longer, and still longer intervals. Then it became silent – and stayed that way. Quite illogically I would check the telephone exchange to see if my phone was out of order. My wife thought I was losing my marbles and she might have been right.

I had been dreaming about telephones when suddenly I was awakened by the sound of the real phone ringing and I went down the stairs two at a time to snatch up the receiver.

"Mr Moss?" came the polite voice.

"Yes!!"

"Could you possibly change your dental appointment to later in the day, please?"

I stared at the phone – it seemed to be grinning at me. It was within an ace of being strangled by its own cord.

I realised that the telephone had been trying to convey a message for a long time. That there has to come a day – for all of us – when the phone stops ringing."

APPENDICES

Appendix 1 – Sidemen and Vocalists

If I were to include all the various musicians such as Max Goldberg that were Jewish, this book would double in size, but it was the bandleaders who drove the Golden Age. However, during my research I came across these people time after time, so I felt that they should have a little Appendix all of their own.

They all tell stories of their own, beginning with Billy Amstell

Billy Amstell, Saxophone

Billy Amstell died in 1906, and what follows is his obituary from the Guardian, written by Peter Vacher.

To listen to the saxophonist and clarinettist Billy Amstell, who has died aged 94, reminisce about the 1930s was to dip into a lost social world - centred on the Prince of Wales and Mrs Simpson - dancing the night away in glitzy hotels and clubs. In 1931 Billy had joined Bert Ambrose's orchestra, arguably the finest British dance band of that decade, which played for the upper-crust at the May Fair Hotel and the Embassy Club, and, in summer followed them to Cannes and Monte Carlo.

In addition, with Ambrose, there were regular broadcasts, frequent recordings and film appearances. It was during those Ambrose years that Billy made the transition from alto to tenor saxophone and created an effective solo style, honing his jazz at late-night venues such as Kate Meyrick's 43 Club at 43 Gerrard Street - where he met Coleman Hawkins.

Billy's parents were Jews from Warsaw who settled in Jamaica Street in Stepney where his father rose to be foreman of a local boot factory. The youngest of seven children, Billy recalled that his father kept the family (including his grandmother) on a wage of £1 per week. Music was encouraged, an elder brother, Mick, dabbled with the drums, while Billy tackled the piano. Eventually both turned to the saxophone and Billy, aged 14, joined Darcy's Baby Band, which despite two of its players being well into their 20s, was billed as the "only juvenile syncopated orchestra in existence". Two years and a Glasgow pantomime engagement later, the Babes were no more.

Back in London and with his brother's help, he took casual dance band gigs and then played with Herman Darewski and Charles Watson, at top locations such as the Piccadilly Hotel and the Kit Kat Club. Billy, self-taught, practised constantly. He explained his early success, saying, "I could read (music) like the very devil."

Then, after 18 months in Glasgow with Watson, he was hired by the American Jack Harris for what Billy described as "a typical society band of the 1930s, playing sweet music in a rather sedate manner" for a residency at the Grosvenor House Hotel. The band recorded some 50 titles and Billy also recorded with vocalist Al Bowlly and recorded and performed with Roy Fox's band. Then came Ambrose. Filming at Pinewood in 1937, Billy met Tessa Gee, an aspiring actress and photographic model; they married a year later but in 1940 came his wartime call-up.

RAF service took him to the Shetlands where he led a small swing group, playing clarinet. Invalided out after a breakdown, Billy resumed his career, first with Geraldo and then with Ambrose again.

In later years, he freelanced, broadcasting regularly with Stanley Black's BBC orchestra and leading his quintet for jazz gigs, by now exclusively on clarinet.

His lively autobiography, Don't Fuss, Mr Ambrose was published in 1986, and he contributed carefully researched articles to Nostalgia magazine. A lively raconteur with a good line in Jewish jokes, Billy was a stalwart of the Coda Club, happy in the company of his many musician friends. "It's marvellous when you earn money and you have fun,"he said.

Before he died he was interviewed by BBC Radio 3 in 2003 for their series *Musicians' Stories*

Here is what he says. IT gives an insight into how the sons of immigrants got into the Dance Band Era.

How I came to this music:

My father, mother and grandmother came to England from Warsaw at the start of the 20th century and settled in Jamaica Street in Stepney. I was the youngest of seven.

If you possessed the musical talent it was a natural thing to do to become a musician, your parents' wishes didn't have much to do with it. My first instrument was piano and I got two certificates from the London College of Music in the west end and my piano teacher was a charming old man. He was a lovely guy and he was heart broken when my mother told him that I was going to play saxophone. You see my brother, Mick, bought he a saxophone and naturally it was kept in the house. When he was out chasing 'birds' - he was a good-looking guy - I would open up his saxophone case and have a blow and my sister would sing the notes for me.

I had a good start because I played the piano, so I had no problem in reading music. And later I used to deputise for guys - just go in sit down, open the book and play- that was no trouble for me at all. Whenever my brother Mick carelessly double-booked himself, he used to send me along. Now I was always short when I was a kid and another brother of mine had to carry my saxophone for me. We'd get to say Hoxton Town Hall (what a joint!) we'd play and they couldn't understand how a kid like me could read orchestrations. I mean they were written tonic sol-fa but these guys couldn't understand how a youngster like that (I was only 14) could do it.

There was a guy in our neighbourhood, his name was Moshe. I did some gigs for him and recorded some of the tunes from those days on the LP that I made in the 1980's. And after I did a gig for him he would come round the next day and give my mother 10 shillings for the gig and a sixpence because I was a good boy. He didn't actually teach me the repertoire (for weddings and barmitzvahs). They played it and I picked it up because I've got a keen ear. We played tunes for any simcha (ie.festivity) and the people there made up their own dances - they did their own thing and they enjoyed it, it wasn't something they had learned from the old people.

Where I play:

Billy Amstelll used to be the soloist in the legendary Ambrose's band in the 30's, and later with the bands of Geraldo and Stanley Black. I'm 91 now but I still enjoy playing.

A favourite song:

'Boobala' (Grandma Dear)

A lot of the tunes were in D minor, a favourite key for Jewish music. I tried to vary it, C Minor say, because it's monotonous, finishing one song in D minor and starting the next in the same key.

Ivor Mairants (guitar player with Geraldo's and Ted Heath's bands) sat in that chair and told me it was 'Ich Bin A Boarder Bay Mein Weib'. But recognising these tunes can be confusing. When I got the master tape back from the studios, after the sessions for the LP, they asked me to name each tune and I couldn't! Ivor 's wife said 'You wrote the arrangements, you played so beautifully…well you're a clever boy and yet…. you don't know the names of the tunes?' So I played her this tune Boobala and at the end I said to her, 'Do you remember that tune from the old days?" and she said "Course I do Billy'. I said 'But Lily, I wrote it for this LP.'

* Billy Amstell's Jewish Party with Harold Berens (Zodiac ZR1015 - recorded 1981) Boobala from that album, features Neil Fullerton on trumpet, Emilio on accordion, Art Learner on bass, Harry Barnett on guitar, Brian Emney on drums and Billy Amstell on clarinet.

Alan Kane, Vocals

Culled from his obituary in the Independent 1996:

Alan Kane was born in the East End of London, at Dalston, in 1913. His father was cantor at the Jubilee Street Synagogue in Whitechapel, which prompted Alan to join the choir of the Chapel Lane Synagogue in Dalston. Leaving school at the age of 14, he soon turned part-time professional.

Having learned to play the drums, Kane formed his own small combination, a dance music quartet. For a few pounds shared between them they would play and sing the night away at many a working men's club around the East End.

When Lew Stone's top vocalist, Al Bowlly, left to go freelance, Stone cast his ears around for a suitable successor and swiftly signed the up-and-coming crooner, 21-year-old Alan Kane. He never quite made it to the top, and certainly never replaced Al Bowlly in the affections of the listening public. However, his pleasant vocalising was worth hearing.

In 1939 he joined ENSA and in 1941 was with Harry Leader, and had a number of wartime hits.

He was a great radio favourite and was heard to effect as a solo singing star on such BBC series as *Break For Music* and the lunch-time variety show, *Workers' Playtime*. In his later years Kane was the musical director at the Wellington Club in Kensington, a position he held for a quarter of a century. After retirement he worked for the charity Operation Wheelchair.

Max Bacon, Drummer

Sourced from Wikipedia and the Jewish Museum

Max Bacon was a real enigma. He was born British – in the East End in 1901, but you would never guess it with his mittel-European accent, and talk laced with Yiddishisms. Not for him dissimulation. He was a full frontal Jew.

Earlier in this book I mentioned Jewface – the comedy Jew - and Bacon was a past master at it. He made a good living out of it. His song *Beigels* is somewhat of a classic, and pines for the good old Whitechapel days, and he also recorded *Gershwin Lokshen-Soup Jack; Beigels; Bar mitzvah boy; Shmoul, Pick up the Kishke; I can get it for you wholesale; Even a Crooner must eat.*

He was described in *Tales of the Savoy: Stories from a Glasgow Café* by Joe Pieri as a "giant of a man with a pleasant rasping voice whose solo act featured prominently in the band's repertoire"; but he would have been as the comedy act, not as an instrumentalist.

All this belied his talent as a drummer – he actually wrote a book on how to drum. An article on the Jewish Museum website states that "Bacon raised the bar for solos and instrumentals in British jazz between the wars." He was truly a man of many talents, so let's leave it to the Jewish Museum:

"His acting debut was in *The Playboy* (1938) alongside Bert Ambrose. On stage he appeared at the Phoenix Theatre with Perlita Neilson and Miriam Karlin in *The Diary of Anne Frank* (1956). Screen roles included *The Entertainer* (1960) as Charlie Klein opposite Sir Laurence Olivier, an episode of the long-running TV series *Z Cars* (1964) and appearing as Mr Fish in *The Whisperers*

(1967), before he appeared in his biggest film, *Chitty Chitty Bang Bang*, the following year."

Wow!

There are no recordings of his later work in film and TV, which is a pity.

He died in 1969.

Harry Lewis

One of those names that crops up continuously when researching the Golden Age, he can inevitably be described as Mr Vera Lynn, being married to the songstress for over 50 years.

Lewis himself had an interesting career. Born (of course) in the East End, he could be described as a journeyman sax and clarinetist playing in various bands, most notably in Ambrose's band in 1939.

It was here that Lynn met Lewis. She said of him that he was "terribly good looking, with a fine head of hair, even if he was rather short.". He played with the Ambrose band, and then when war came he joined up and went into the RAF to form the 'The Royal Air Force Dance Orchestra', otherwise known as the Squadronnaires.

We are told that he left the Squadronnaires around 1943. He was only 27, but it seems that he gave up his career to manage Vera Lynn which he then did until his death in 1998. We have already seen that the life of a musician was peripatetic, to say the least. Perhaps he felt that his marriage meant more than his career

Lew Davis, Trombonist

Lew Davis was one of those sidemen whose names keep cropping up all the time, and that is because he was clearly one of the best, if not **the** best trombonist of the 1930s. He was an integral part of Jack Hyltons outfit – it was said that "any trombone heard on Hylton records from that time is almost certainly Lew Davis"

He played with Jack Hylton, Ray Noble, Ambrose, and then Lew Stone, all top bandleaders.

As mentioned, according to Lew Stone's biography it was he who persuaded Stone to record the Yiddish song *A Brivele der Mamen* in the 1930s.

Harry Gold

Harry Gold, like Lew Davis, is one of those characters that crops up again and again.

His obituary in the Guardian by John Fordham states that: "A prolific bandleader, musician and arranger, he was at the heart of the jazz world for more than 70 years.

He was also a tenacious campaigner for jazz recognition, inside and outside the music business. In the 1940s, he was one of a small group of jazz musicians to shift the Musicians' Union policy over pay rates away from its classical bias. He loved playing all his life, and relished any opportunity at any age."

He was born Hyman Goldberg in Leytonstone in 1907; and to cut a long story short learnt a variety of instruments at the London College of Music, before embarking on a career as a musician in the early 1920s. He then played with a variety of bandleaders, notably Ambrose and Geraldo, and with Roy Fox from 1932 to 1937.

He had strong socialist tendencies, reinforced by playing at the posh clubs where he is said to have seen the contrast in poverty and wealth in the country in sharper focus, and from that time was active in union activities, in the end falling out with Fox over rates of pay.

During the war he developed a band with Oscar Rabin's setup that came to be known as Harry Gold's Pieces of Eight - Dixieland jazz style, with various line-ups, until its leader's last years.

An amazing story is told in his obituary: "The group also almost became one of the earliest British bands to perform on television when the Alexandra Palace broadcasting station went on air again in 1946. Their number was pulled because the producer refused to allow Gold's black trombonist, Geoff Love, and the band's white singer, Jane Lee, to perform a duet together on television. "

Given what had happened with Nat Bookbinder, we should not be surprised.

Over the years he would re-form his Pieces of Eight on a regular basis, and occasionally tour, a jazz virtuoso. He died in 2005.

Sam Browne. Vocalist

For a brief time, the singing voice of Sam Browne came back into the public eye, having been forgotten for many years. When the Dennis Potter classic *The Singing Detective* was made, they used some of his songs in it.

He was described as quintessentially British, but like others with Jewish ancestry who have had that description such as Leslie Howard, it was only a mask.

From *The Ballad Years From the Bombs to the Beatles: a Directory and Discography of British Popular Music-makers from 1945-1960, Volumes 1-3 - Don Wicks 1996:*

"He was born in 1898 in East London (where else) to Lithuanian Jewish parents, (TZ note: but they must have moved pretty sharpish because his father had a shoemaker's shop near Tottenham Hotspur Football Club and Sam became a lifelong supporter). At 18 during the First World War, he joined the Merchant Navy. It was on visits to New York that he discovered "iazz" and developed an ambition to become a musician himself.

Back home and on dry land once again Sam bought a drum kit and with a couple of like-minded souls on piano and guitar formed the Tottenham Dance Band, gaining a few bookings around North London halls. As they became more successful other instruments were added and Sam introduced his vocal contribution which came to be the mainstay of the outfit, resulting in a booking at Stockholm Casino that lasted a year.

After this success Sam decided to go solo and found work mainly around various London clubs. Jack Hylton took him up. Sam, always a natty dresser with a voice described as "ball bearing smooth", was an asset to any leader, being a rarity among vocalists, a sight reader, able to sing any song straight off the written music.

After two years of travelling, Sam opted for a more settled life joining Ambrose at London`s May Fair Hotel, later moving with them to Ciro's and to the Embassy club, while also doing variety, recording and broadcasting work. Sam stayed with Ambrose until the outbreak of World War II when, classified as medically unfit for service, he joined ENSA and entertained the troops at home and abroad.

Times were good and with earnings up to £35,000 (ITM) a week he moved with his second wife Olga (his first wife Terry had died in 1931) and two daughters through a succession of luxury homes. No stranger to racecourses and gambling, Sam also loved playing golf.

Sam re-joined Jack Hylton for a special 'Band That Jack Built' feature on the 1950 Royal Variety Show. But a new younger generation of crooners were taking over in the 1950s.

Despite the occasional variety tour, Sam`s finances became tight, putting a strain on his marriage and it broke up in 1955. A night club venture and voice training school had both folded and by the latter part of the decade Sam was reduced to living in a small central London flat. With no singing work he took a job for a time as a clerk in a betting shop, but this came to grief and he eventually finished up in a North London basement bedsit. Ill health finally overtook him and he died from cancer at Highgate Hospital on 2nd March 1972, virtually forgotten. He is buried at Rainham Jewish cemetery.

For someone who was at the very top of his profession, his story is particularly tragic.

Ray Ellington, Vocalist

Of a different character and background was Ray Ellington, bandleader, jazz singer, drummer. At some point in *The Goon Show*, the plot would move almost seamlessly into a jazz number by Ellington, usually with him singing a jazz standard, rarely anything to do with the storyline. His band would often play alongside Max Geldray, also Jewish.

His association with the Goon Show gave him lasting and permanent fame.

What is almost unknown are his Jewish roots

He was born as Henry Pitts Brown in London of an American father (a music hall comedian and entertainer), and Russian (and Jewish) mother, Eva Rosenthal.

His father died when he was four and his mother brought him up in the Orthodox tradition; he once said that his mother made him lay tefillin every morning, and he attended the South London Jewish School in Elephant and Castle until he was 14, when he became an apprentice cabinet maker.

He soon went into the entertainment business, playing the drums and singing until finally he joined Harry Roy and His Orchestra in 1937. He called himself Ellington after his hero, Duke Ellington.

After the war he played with other bands but in 1947 formed his own quartet and soon after joined *The Goon Show*.

Charles 'Nat' Star, Recording Artist

Charles 'Nat' Star (aka Nat Star) does not easily fit into any category. As a sideman he performed at many 'gigs, but was never contracted to any one location, or one bandleader, and was more of a recording artist than a live dance band musician or bandleader. There is no doubt that he was influential and played with many of the top stars of the day.

His life has been documented by Terry Brown, researcher and discographer, in an article called "Charles Nat Star – A life in music", and what follows is sourced from that material.

Naftali Hirsch Starsolla, later called Charles 'Nat' Star, was born in Poland in 1886 and came to South London in 1900, aged 4. For family reasons, he was sent to the Jewish Hospital and Orphan Asylum, which by 1900 came under the Department of Education. It later became better known as the Norwood Home for Jewish Children. in South London. The 'Asylum' ran music classes which enabled the growing Nat Star to learn clarinet and saxophone.

After leaving, he became apprenticed as a cabinet-maker, and for years this seems to have been his main occupation, but not his favourite, because according to later family research he also seemed to have been earning a few crumbs as a semi-professional musician playing at the Yiddish Theatre, and no doubt at the odd Bar Mitzvah and wedding.

It is important to understand that he was an earlier generation than the likes of Ambrose, Stone, Lipton, Phillips, and Winnick, He treaded a path that few had gone. Whereas for the above mentioned individuals, there seemed to be a natural progression to dance band leadership, for him a much rougher path. He was in essence leading the way.

In any case by the time we get to 1920, he has had a spell in the Territorial Army, is married and settled and playing as a regular at Ciro's. He was obviously well regarded, evidenced by the fact that the Prince of Wales once asked Nat to teach him the saxophone. As a sign of his regard in the business was that he was invited to play with Jack Hylton

He was only with Hylton for a short time, but even by the early twenties, Hylton was a megastar, and only the best was good enough for Jack. He joined late 1921 (ish) with Hylton's 'Queen's Dance Orchestra', which played on the roof garden of the Queens Hall in London's Langham Place

It was with Hylton that Nat began his recording career, playing on around 60 sides for HMV and Zonophone (HMV's budget label.

As mentioned earlier in the book Hylton loved the variety circuit, and found touring highly profitable. Even the 'Queen's Dance Orchestra' was not rooted to one place. It played at a variety of locations with maybe the highlight of its existence being its appearance at the influential Daily Express Woman's Exhibition at Olympia, which ran in July 1922.

Star left Hylton in November 1922, having been with him for less than a year. One can guess that the punishing schedule that Hylton demanded of his sidemen may have played a part. By 1922 Star was 36 with a wife and family. Hylton, on the other hand was 30, Harry Roy was 22, Bert Ambrose 28. It was a young man's game.

Also maybe the most important thing that he gained from his time from Hylton was a love of the recording studio – and perhaps, like many modern musicians, he found that it was there that he had the best chance to express himself artistically, as opposed to the sweaty, overcrowded environment of the ballroom, with its many excessive demands on the musician.

To cut a long story short, Star became more and more involved with session work. That is not to say that he didn't perform with dance bands – one contract with a band called The London Band lasted 30 weeks from 1924 to 1925, and paid £1500/week (ITM), but it must be pointed out at just one location, the Hippodrome.

Terry Brown states that from here on in, , "Nat's studio based recording activities began to burgeon, to say the least. Presumably Nat, as per usual, fitted in his, 'live' work with his recording sessions as and when he could................ up to this point in time, Nat had been principally playing as a session man and musician for hire"

One might say that by 1925 Star was at the top of his profession. He was admired by all, played with the top musicians of the time –

Jack Hylton was happy to re-employ him when the opportunity came, and over next few years (simplifying things somewhat for brevity) he played with many bands, had a studio based dance band, organised other bands in the recording studio, and became Musical Director for Homochord's Sterno Records, a budget label. He played and produced some of the famous names in the business

Yet by 1934 with Sterno Records failing, and as Terry Brown tells us, "no doubt exhausted" he changed direction, and opened a radio and electrical shop 'Star Radio' in East London, aided by his son, Bert. He was 48.

He continued to play and conduct, either as a sideman, or with a put together band notably for a short period with Radio Luxembourg, but he focused more and more on his shop.

Terry Brown tells us that it appears that dementia set in the 1940s. Today we would probably call it early onset Alzheimers, and he died in March 1950 at only 63 years of age.

In summary, Terry tells us that "Charles Nat Star was an important and highly talented British musician who majored in reed instruments….he pioneered the potential of the saxophone as a dance band instrument, and as such, he remained much in demand performing with some of the best dance bands of the day. Nat also led and organized many studio based recording bands and became one of an elite group of studio band musicians constantly in demand for recording work"

So why did he not reach the pinnacle?

His age must have counted against him. He was up against much younger people that him, but John Wright, another researcher of those days, suggests there were other reasons:

- He had a poor choice of record labels. He became a big fish in a small pond with Sterno records, whose facilities were substandard, and who spent very little money on promotion, and who ultimately failed.
- He never built up a cadre of sidemen. When the famous Ted Heath played with Nat's band, it was not his 'day job'
- Too many times he recorded under an assumed name – so people never got to know him as a name. As John Wright said "record company chose to use over thirty different pseudonyms which bewildered record buyers at the time and they would rarely associate Homochord or Sterno records with the bandleader Nat Star"

I believe this last point hits the spot. To reach the top, talent as a musician is not enough. As we saw with Ambrose, Roy, or even Maurice Winnick, brand was and is to this day, all important. Nat Star was one of the hardest workers, he was inspirational, talented, but because he never went on tour, and without his name on billboards (there may be exceptions) people never learnt his name; because he was never associated with a leading hotel or restaurant, or dance hall, he never built up the high level contacts that would get him the recording contracts with HMV, or a gig at the Blackpool Tower Ballroom

Of course, it is always possible that Nat never wanted what the others had and was happy with his lot in life. Maybe he didn't want to conduct dance bands on the circuit, or at the Savoy. He had a family life, and as an older man maybe that was good enough for him.

Appendix 2 – The Album

If I was making an album of tunes from the bandleaders, this would be my playlist. They are all available on YouTube.

My favourite? Sam Browne. *Cream in My Coffee,* followed closely by *My Woman.*

Ambrose	The Continental
Ambrose	Who's been Polishing the Sun
Harry Roy	Leicester Square Rag
Harry Roy	Swing for Sale (Ray Ellington)
Max Bacon	Beigels
Lew Stone	A Brivele der Mamen
Harry Roy	She Had to Go and Lose it at the Astor
Lew Stone	My Woman
Geraldo	That Lovely Weekend
Johnny Rosen	My Bluebird
Joe Loss	March of the Mods
Joe Loss	Wheels Cha Cha
Nat Temple	Nattering Around
Sid Phillips	I Found a New Baby
Oscar Rabin	See How They Run
Syd Lipton	Looking on the Bright Side
Jack Hylton (Sam Browne)	You're the Cream in My Coffee (Sam
Al Bowlly	Bei Mir Bist du Schon
Ambrose	Jeepers Creepers

Appendix 3 – "Izzy Azzy Wozz"

Now Mr Izzy Rubenstein, who was very old,
One day playing tiddly-winks, he caught a nasty cold.
His great-great-grandson wrapped him up and put him into bed,
His lawyer called next morning, and this is what he said:

'Oh, is Mr Izzy ill? Izzy? Izzy?
Will he make a will? Will he? Will he?
I am Izzy's lawyer and I'm calling round because
I want to know is Izzy ill, or Izzy as he was?'

Now no-one tried to answer him, unto his dismay,
The lawyer's face went very pale as he was heard to say,
'I've been in charge of his affairs since 1862,
He owes me six and eightpence, so tell me quickly, do:
Oh, is Mr Izzy ill? Izzy? Izzy?
Has he caught a chill? Has he? Has he?
The slightest cold often turns to 'flu,
Appendicitis, tonsillitis and bronchitis too.
Is he breathing still? Is he? Is he?
I am Izzy's lawyer and I'm calling round because
I want to know is Izzy ill, or Izzy as he was?'

Appendix 4 – When Harry met Gracie

This is also in my other book, but because the eras match, it is too good to leave out – and it is about the songwriters, without whom the bandleaders would have been nothing. We don't think that they could have been Jewish – but they were – and some came from the East End

This story came completely from left field, and shows if nothing else that there were Jewish songsmiths in Britain in the 1930s who operated at the very top level. Two of them co-wrote one of the most iconic songs in British musical history.

My story began when I was researching a tune called Mazeltov which had been played by the Joe Loss Band in 1939.

A familiar tune which has been played at weddings since time immemorial – or at least since the time when klezmer bands started playing it – is Chosen Kallah Mazeltov. Clearly this pre-dated Joe Loss, whose new song had the following refrain:

Mazel Mazel Mazeltov
That's the best a friend can do
Here's Good Health to Everyone
May the skies always be blue.

The melody is more or less the same as Chosen Kallah Mazeltov, but the words are somewhat different. It was never recorded and all we have is some sheet music, which indicates that he must have played it on occasion, I guess, at weddings and bar mitzvahs – I cannot see it being played at the Astoria Ballroom, Hammersmith or the Ritz.

I was intrigued by this rare tune so I looked up the songsmiths, who happened to be Spencer Williams, Ralph Stanley, and Leo Towers.

There is no trace of a London-based Ralph Stanley that could be our man (I found a Ralph Stanley who lived in Tennessee, but he didn't fit the profile), but what is absolutely gobsmackingly amazing is that one of the men who co-wrote *Mazeltov* is the same Spencer Williams from Selma, Alabama who wrote *Basin Street Blues*.

He was living in London at the time in Sunbury on Thames. I guess that he will have transcribed the music. It is a fact that there was a great deal of cross-cultural activity in the States between Jews and blacks, so it is possible that he may well have heard the 'other' *Mazeltov* before.

The third person was Leo Towers, and that is where the story deepens.

His real name was Leonard Blitz, and he was Jewish, of Dutch origin, born in the East End.

As a solo songwriter his career was rather nondescript. However, he did better when he teamed up with others. Co-writing was not uncommon, or a bad thing, as any fan of Gilbert and Sullivan or Lennon and McCartney will tell you. Another Jewish songwriter, Eric Maschwitz, who wrote the iconic *A Nightingale Sang in Berkeley Square* and *These Foolish Things*, would always team up with others who could provide the music for his lyrics, and indeed did so with Towers for a song called *Mardi Gras*.

Another collaborator for Towers was the bandleader Billy Cotton. Together they wrote *Wakey Wakey*, the theme tune for Cotton's band; but he was at his best when he teamed up with Art Noel, real name Aaron Sugarman, better known as Harry Leon, another East Ender who was born in Spitalfields in 1901.

The pair are best known for the inspiration that Leon had in 1931 when the song he wrote in conjunction with Towers and William E. Haines became recognisably one of the classics of the century.

Richard Baker, in his book *Old Time Variety*, tells us how Leon had been in the Merchant Navy, had left it and managed to get a job playing the piano in a pub. After a while Harry began to compose tunes, which he would then no doubt play for the customers. One ditty he composed was called *Gypsy Sweetheart.*

Baker tells us that Harry at that point couldn't write a note of music. The East End community was very close, and Leon will have known Towers, even been a friend of his. There is no doubt that Towers with his musical background – according to his obituary in the Jewish Chronicle he was a violinist – will have been able to transcribe the music. Towers, we are told, wrote the lyrics to this tune and off they went to a publisher, William E. Haines, who told them bluntly that the song did not sound like a gypsy song, so the lyrics would not do.

This sounds to me as though Haines loved the tune but hated the lyrics, so they worked on them in Haines' office, first of all calling the song "Mary, Mary", with the lyrics "Mary, Mary, don't be contrary" (try it out – it fits!), but finally settled on the nickname of Leo's sister Sarah – Sally.

One nice story is that they got stuck on what would rhyme with the word 'smiling', and another songwriter, Percy Edgar, stuck his head round the door and said "what about beguiling?".

There are two alternate histories from now on.
The first is that the three of them took the song to Gracie Fields, who turned it down, but on learning shortly afterwards that she was about to be in a film called "Sally in our Alley", Fields called them back, and the song was written into the film.

The other version comes from Fields' biography. Whilst backstage
at The Metropolitan, Fields recounted, "In comes this fellow one
night, very Cockney, and he tells us all of this song he's just written
with some friends. The title of the song was *Sally*." It seems like an
example of synchronicity, for the name of her new film was not
public yet – but what a bonus! After her manager Archie Pitt had a
listen, it was used in the film over six times and wherever Gracie
Fields went in later life, the song went with her.

Fields claimed in later life that she wanted to "Drown blasted Sally
with Walter with the aspidistra on top!", a reference to her well-
known songs *Walter, Walter,* and *The Biggest Aspidistra In The
World.*

Sally turned out to be her swan song. In 1978 she appeared
as a surprise guest in the finale of the Royal Variety Performance
and sang *Sally*, remarking that all her life she had been singing a
man's song. It was to be her final public appearance. She died in
1979.

As for the songsmith, Leo Towers, it seems he had a fairly
comfortable life, and was well respected. He was musical director of
Moss and Stoll Theatres, whose portfolio included the Lyric, Garrick
and the famous London Palladium. He was also quite a prolific
songwriter, and so popular that in later life he was voted Life Vice
President of the Songwriters' Guild for all the work he had done to
improve the lot of the songwriter, who was often, to put it in the
vernacular, "ripped off ". He died in 1973.

Harry Leon, it seems, did not have it so good. He had missed out on
millions by selling his share of *Sally* for £30, worth around £2,000
today – which would seem a reasonable amount of money to
someone who was making a living playing in pubs. Perhaps his
'friends' could have advised him better.

He had a number of hits later on, writing light entertainment songs,
the best known of which were *The Barrow Boy Song,* and especially

Kiss me Goodnight, Sergeant Major, with which Arthur Askey, the Liverpudlian comedian, had a hit.

One of the songs he co-wrote with Towers was "My Heart's in Old Killarney" (1936) which includes the lyrics: "When I dream of old Ireland, land of my birth…that land where the green shamrock grows", which is not bad for two East End Jews. I hasten to point out that George Gershwin wrote about the Swanee river, although he had never visited Georgia.

However, it seems that Leon spent all the money he had earned. He ended up quite bitter, went bankrupt in 1954, and died in1968 in virtual poverty.

Richard Baker recounts how Leon "could be seen most lunchtimes in a pub near Denmark Street wearing a cloth cap and a muffler, and smoking Woodbines from a gold cigarette case".

Mavis Steel, in The Jewish East End of London website, tells of his latter years.

"Harry was living in a transport cafe in Kentish Town in 1966, where I worked. He was very down and out and everyone knew him. He played piano in local pubs for drinks. He used to come down in the mornings when he heard me start work and often he would say put my tea and toast 'on the book', and I often let it go. He said he had written for Gracie Fields and he said that if he had all the money that was owing to him he would be a rich man."

In people's minds *Sally* became an anthem for the working people of England. Who could have guessed that it had been written by two East London Jews?

Appendix 5 – The Time of My Life – Eamonn Andrews

Introduction

I was giving old Punch magazines a scan before throwing them into the paper waste, when I came across this article written by Eamonn Andrews in April 1975.

He was a well-loved TV presenter, sports commentator, and an A-List celebrity from the 1950s - 1980s who pioneered the talk show host format in the UK, and was noted for two shows: *What's My Line,* and *This is Your Life*, a British biographical show, both of which had top rating.

It is a snapshot of an era, of his life and of dance bands on the road. So, as they say, over to Eamonn:

The Time of my Life

It was when I joined a dance band.

More precisely, it was when I joined Joe Loss and his Orchestra in a strictly non-musical capacity, and it probably needs some slight explanation.

I was working in Dublin's Theatre Royal. My job was to present a giveaway quiz called *Double or Nothing*. Visiting top-of-the-ball was Joe Loss, who saw the quiz and invited me to join up for three months on his pre-summer tour of Britain, presenting the quiz as part of his superlatively professional theatre show.

I was over the moon with excitement. I had been trying for years to break down the monolithic and monopolistic BBC without a tremor of success. Now I would be on their doorstep. Under their very noses. They would see the treasures of talent they had been spurning by letter, by phone call, by duplicated circular. Then came the official approach from Joe's distinguished agent. Whoever heard of an agent?

He offered me £40 a week (£1400 ITM)........Days, weeks months – I have no idea for how long the time machine twirled, then I was on a plane, twenty pounds in my pocket, a case, a tuxedo, a spare pair of socks and within a few hours the mysteries of Regent Street and an extraordinary man with a hunted look, slightly humped back, an aggressive, deceptive front, spectacles, faintly clicking front teeth, an English accent, and the name, Dan Treacy.

I was yet to meet the saxes and the trombones and the drums that would explain why Dan kept putting out the kind light in his eye.

He was the road manager. He was the one that got the band from city to city. Most of all, he was the man who saw to it that all the members of the team arrived on time and compos mentis. He was a brave man.

Within days I had stepped into a mad, self-contained, swift-moving, exhilarating, bewildering caravanserai. We were on what was known as the Moss Empire circuit. I was about to be educated from Shepherds Bush to Glasgow. I didn't even faintly realise it, but I was on a crash course in one of the universities of show business. Within three months, I was going to learn a lot of things that might otherwise have taken twenty years, or never.

My professors were all top professional musicians, being paid more than I was, to provide the super big band shows that Joe Loss wanted, and to accept the discipline that lesser outfits would never have tolerated. Birds were banned, booze was frowned on, rules were only bent with discretion, and, if a player stepped over whatever the invisible line was, he disappeared without trace as if the KGB had plucked him away to the cold craw of silent Siberia.

I was fair game and gauche, and I quickly discovered that your leg is only as long as you let it be.

In Manchester, three of the lads took me to a small but popular Jewish restaurant called Blacks and introduced me to the delights of chopped liver, roll-mop herring, and gefilte fish. The fish was a heavenly dish to my untutored palate. Next day I said I was going back for lunch to have more of the fish dish, the name of which I had already forgotten. No-one would come with me but they gave me the address and told me to go up to the counter and request a double helping of meshugga fish. The silence that fell in the area around me gave me no clue that I was asking for a non-existing dish (translated as mad fish). I seem to remember leaving when I saw the proprietor reaching for the telephone.

The days rolled by with work and play and digs of all shapes and sizes………

Last date as I remembered it was the Alhambra, Bradford. The band was off to the Isle of Man for its summer dancing season. The quiz was ended. My university was closing. In a fit of nostalgia I decided to blow my last week's wages on a farewell drink for my professors.

Joe gave me permission to give the boys a modest glass or two in the hotel across the road from the stage door. The only possible time was between first and second house, Saturday night…….The farewell drinks went the way farewell drinks go – down. I failed to spot that Sammy, the saxophone player, who was going through the aches of unrequited love….had already hit a first house bottle or two…..

Thirty minutes later, Joe Loss bounced on stage in front of his impeccable orchestra as In the Mood elasticated the proscenium arch. On one of his conducting pirouettes he spotted Sammy, green and gagging over his silent sax.

Sacrilege.

Joe hissed him off stage and Sammy stumbled into the darkness……..

Show over, Joe in a lather of sweat and rage brushed by my protestations of innocence and slammed into his dressing toom followed by manager Dan Treacy, purple at the prospect of the imminent execution. Sammy's career was over.

Only a drunk could have saved him, and did. Sammy went to Joe's dressing room, threw open the door, held onto the knob, and slurred out three momentous words.

"Joe, I resign".

The world stood still. Then a sound like sheet metal splitting.

"You'll bloody well resign when I tell you to. Get out! Get out!"

I believe he lasted another six months.

My education was complete.

The Article in Context

As Andrews said in his article, his fame was not ever so, and early he struggled on to be recognised. By 1945 he was having success with Irish Radio, but he was unrecognised outside Ireland, and failed to get the gig he really wanted, a job with the BBC. He had been unsuccessfully barraging the BBC with applications for work for years, and failed.

His fortunes changed when an Irish Jewish entrepreneur, Louis Ellimann, became involved. His father had come from Kovno in Lithuania. According to family tradition he had walked to Hamburg, and instead of taking ship for New York, was persuaded to go to

Dublin, where he became the father of the Dublin film industry. His son Louis, born in 1903, became known as "Ireland's Mr. Showbusiness".

In 1948 Ellimann "engaged Andrews as a stage quiz master before live audiences on '*Double or Nothing*', first at the Savoy cinema in Limerick, and then in the Theatre Royal, Dublin, where he was seen by English bandleader Joe Loss, who signed him to present the quiz as an interlude act on a 1949 British tour."

The rest is history. The BBC was looking for a quiz master to replace the current one for the popular BBC radio programme *Ignorance is Bliss,* created by Maurice Winnick, the ex-bandleader. It was a mock quiz show on which a panel of comedians gave zany responses to simple questions. Having seen him work with Joe Loss they needed look no further than Andrews.

The rest, as they say, (and I say quite often) is history.

Postscript
Well, not quite. The iconic Gaiety Theatre in Dublin, owned by Louis Elliman from 1936, was sold in 1965 to a company owned by Eamonn Andrews. Later the Eurovision Song Contest was broadcast from the Gaiety to a worldwide audience of 400 million. After starting out as a bit act in Dublin and being given his first real break by Elliman, Andrews now had the financial clout to buy one of Elliman's theatres.

What goes around comes around.

References
http://www.arthurlloyd.co.uk/Dublin/GaietyTheatreDublin.htm
http://www.louiselliman.com/
Online Dictionary of Irish Biography

Appendix 6 – The Business of the Dance Band Era

Introduction

All the way through the book I have been mentioning money. Bandleaders and musicians may have loved their jobs, but they were principally there to make money. It was not a hobby.

Some of them were at the very top of the profession, while others struggled to earn a crust – and they operated in a range of environments, from The Savoy to church halls, with different sizes of orchestras, and in different parts of the UK.

As you might expect from that, earnings varied wildly, and the Musicians Union would also put its oar in, trying to enforce minimum wages for its members to avoid the worst excesses of exploitation. It set up a byzantine scale of pay rates where the rate might differ according to the size of hall, the type of instrument being used, and even whether the player was casual or 'permanent'.

Actual information on the pay rates of bandleaders and their sidemen, including vocalists, is quite sparse, although some writers, notably Albert McCarthy in his final chapter of his book *The Dance Band Era*, have made an attempt at giving concrete figures.

McCarthy stated that bandleaders would often "be unwilling to deny reports of huge earnings, for these could be advantageous in any bargaining with club or hotel managements."

He added "Then, even when what seems a spectacular fee for a date turns out to be, for once, correct, there may have been special circumstances governing its payment. One such example is a reported fee of £83,000 for the Ambrose band to play a week at the Glasgow Empire Exhibition in May 1938, which would be atypical."

McCarthy maybe ignored that in 1923 Ambrose was enough of a pull financially to earn £600,000 from the May Fair Hotel, so perhaps that was not so atypical for Ambrose.

What follows is a summary of some of the information uncovered or deduced by McCarthy and others, to give you an idea of the financial environment that these people operated in. I have 'converted' 1920s and 1930s monies into 'today's monies' using the *Cost of Living* website. The results are not exact, but are close enough to give a ballpark figure, which I have rounded up or down.

The Musicians

I'll start off with a musician: Nat Star, who we met earlier.

Terry Brown, writing in November 2018, looked at contracts signed by Nat, which showed how much a top musician could expect to earn.

He was contracted to play at Ciro's Club with the Ciro Orchestra for £1100 per week in February 1922, and booked for four weeks, so his month's earning would have been around £4,400. It was seven days a week and he worked five hours every night (instead of the contracted two). It is equivalent to a daily rate of around £160, and an hourly rate of around £30. The pay of £1100 may have sounded impressive, but he certainly worked for it!

Terry suggests that this could have been a 'dep' contract, where someone stands in for a regular, which might suggest that 'normal' rates for a musician were somewhat less.

He had a second spell at Ciro's, this time at £1400 a week. He had obviously learnt his lesson about the trustworthiness of the management, and would extract every drop.

It was not only management that would seek to keep musicians' wages down. It was also in the bandleader's interests. The £83,000 that Ambrose earned in Glasgow was not a net figure, but gross. Out of that figure he would be expected to pay his musicians - and bandleaders would often find themselves also paying supporting acts.

Ambrose may have been a top earner, but enjoyed success because he paid top dollar. In 1930 he tempted Sid Phillips to join his band with an offer of £1600 a week.

Unsurprisingly there were constant disputes. In 1938 Geraldo, then in residence at the Savoy Hotel, was faced by an ultimatum from the Musicians' Union: unless he increased their salaries to conform to the minimum of £700 a week they would order the musicians not to resume work.

Harry Leader also had a dispute, and one which explains why he was not popular in some quarters. In July 1939 he fell foul of the union over his payments to 15 musicians for a dance date at Folkestone, involving three hours' playing time. His original offer of £160 a man (with expenses) failed to meet the union minimum of £270. His solution was to drop five members of the personnel and pay the £270 fee to the 10 he retained. This cannot have made him popular!

Johnny Rosen, after he left Jack Hylton, attempted to set up a band in London but found London wage rates were too high for the sort of money he personally could pull in, so he moved North, and chose to use Liverpool musicians instead - pay rates being lower in the North West than in London.

We know how much Johnny Rosen's band members were paid for his time at Lewis's Department Stores in Liverpool, as he was forced to explain his rates during his bankruptcy case. They were paid £425 per week, which was probably in line with union rates.

These weekly components do not give us the big picture as to what a musician might earn in a year. However, Roy Fox's 1936 wage bill

for his band does. It amounted to £2,100,000, which translates to
£40,000 per week. By any measure this is not small beer .
Fox wouldn't accept an engagement for less than £42,000 a week,
which looks as though it would cover his wage bill at least, but gives
him no margin for personal profit. However he often charged higher
than £42,000 and took a percentage of receipts. By the way, this
indicates that the dance halls' gross income from him was well
above that figure.

The records show that in 1936 the lowest-paid musician in his band
received a weekly salary of £900, while the highest received £1600
per week. These are very high wages indeed. Geraldo had invited
trouble by only paying his sidemen £700 per week, and Rosen only
paid £450 a week.

At one time Fox employed a total of 21 musicians (including
vocalists and an orchestrator), and if this demonstrates anything, it
is that at the top, key individuals made good money. However,
these amounts are not excessive and insane, and do not account
for any additional earnings from radio or recording that the sidemen
might have been making. A performer could earn around £3000 a
week from work in a regular band, recording and broadcasting fees
- and I assume superstars such as Al Bowlly earned even more.

The Bandleaders

At his bankruptcy hearing, Johnny Rosen stated that he was used
to earning £70,000 a year. I believe this to be on the low side (after
all, you would be keen to play down your earnings in such
circumstances), for he not only played at Lewis's Department
Stores, where he personally earned £1500 a week, but toured the
North West with his band, released records, and occasionally
appeared on the radio.

This defensiveness was apparent when Joyce Stone discussed her
husband's 'books' with McCarthy, notwithstanding that she had
some of Lew's payment books to back up her assertions.

She was defensive about the massive payments to band leaders such as the £83,000 to Ambrose, and stated that although sums like £42,000 and £56,000 might be bandied about as weekly payments for the services of a leading 1930s band, she said that they weren't the whole story. She said that "the mere size of the clubs and hotel rooms in which the bands performed would make them unlikely".

She gave McCarthy an example of Lew Stone at the Trianon in 1938, asserting that it was somewhere near the norm.

- Lew Stone had a 12-piece band. He charged £18,000 per week. He paid the band at a weekly rate of £800 as a maximum.
- Taking those figures into account, the weekly wage bill for the band was £800x12 = £9,600.
- Therefore Lew Stone's net takings were £18,000- £9,600 = £8,400.
- If one extrapolates over a year, it's the equivalent of £420,000 per year, six times Rosen's earnings.

The Top End

By the late 1930s Lew Stone was at the top of his game and a high earner. He would be working most of the year, and would be supplementing earnings from live music with radio and with recording. He was also a top-class arranger, which would further add to his income.

In my opinion, Stone's gross turnover just from live music would be a minimum of around £1 million. It's my view that Joyce, who had quite a socialist leaning, did not want to be seen as a 'fat cat', and so played down the massive earnings her husband made.

In contrast, Harry Roy had no qualms about stating that in the 1930s he was earning £3,500,000 per year, and we can see that if

Roy Fox had a wage bill of over £2,000,000, then Fox, too, must have had a decent living over and beyond his band's wage bill.

How the bandleaders made these vast amounts of money is best explained by looking at the career of Jack Hylton, who was at the very top of the pile.

- He was offered £2.6 million for a year's contract at the Leicester Square Theatre, but turned it down, because he could earn more touring. According to Peter Faint, in 1926 Hylton played to 1,500,000 people. If you estimate in a worst case scenario that they paid an average of £5 each, that's a lot of revenue for the dance hall, a good proportion of which will have been passed on to Hylton
- He had a 10-week residency at the KitKat Club, where he earned £630,000 while simultaneously broadcasting from there for the BBC, and also played at the Brixton Astoria, where it's estimated he played in front of 63,000 people. Punishing but lucrative
- In 1926 he sold 800,000 records at a profit of £200,000
- He had a contract with Decca worth £3.75 million over two years
- He turned down £150,000/week for a tour of Germany.

To add to this, there were plenty of commercial opportunities for the bandleader and/or musician, such as sheet music or the advertising of products, as can be seen below.

Source of photograph unknown

Coming back to Harry Roy, given that he toured the country, was on the radio, sold records, and appeared in films (which would have been a high earner), £3,500,000 does not seem to be impossible.

The lower end

However, before we get too carried away with talk of millions, average earnings were much less. As a musician you would be fortunate to be included in a recording contract. McCarthy states: "Then, as now, the regular recording musicians were a select band, accounting for only a fraction of even the men who played in the leading orchestras. The leaders clearly had more opportunities for making extra money, apart from the fact that they received the largest individual share of all monies earned in any case.

For the less fortunate musician, unable to make the major bands or find any foothold in the recording or broadcasting studios, the glamour associated with his profession must have seemed a little tawdry at times, for his rewards were only fractionally better than those enjoyed by citizens in more humdrum occupations. The 1930s were indeed the 'golden years' for the dance bands, but for the actual musicians the gold must at times have seemed a mirage."

Provincial musicians were paid much less than their London counterparts, and it must be pointed out that the Golden Age was not only driven by such as Hylton, Ambrose and Geraldo, but also by literally thousands of musicians playing at dance halls from Bolton to Bangor, Dundee to Durham, and Swansea to Southampton – and largely to the 'common man'.

According to Michael Brocken, in Merseyside there were dozens of semi-professional bands or a variety of combinations playing at dance halls of many varieties. Some of these bands will have been well-known locally, but never even came to the attention of the local press.

He stated that there was a 'dance season' from September to April, and bands would play on average five nights per week during this period.

1935 earnings would be £35 per night (some distance from £700 a night!) with an extra bonus of £10 if the dance went on into the wee small hours, so working things out five nights a week would give the artist a minimum weekly income of around £175. The Musicians' Union minimum was £300 per week, so this was well below the rate, but as a clerk's wage averaged out at £90 per week, dance band fees could be a fantastic source of extra cash.

Summary

As McCarthy said: "The tales of vast sums of money earned and lost, and showbiz stories of high living, need to be treated with caution. It is salutary to remember that at least some of the most famous leaders died in circumstances hardly suggesting affluence."

For the vast majority of band leaders and musicians, it was a precarious existence at best, with the chance of being sacked at a moment's notice ever-present.

To the musician, though, it was preferable to working in a factory or an office, and even to this day musicians live with the risks because there is lots of fun to be had, and a chance to express themselves artistically - and for the top people the rewards were definitely there. To chase the buck was a young man's sport, and by the time the 1950s arrived, the young men had turned to rock and roll. My book shows how many gave up bandleading after only a couple of decades and then left the business altogether or went into management.

It was, however, a unique period in British musical history, and for those that rode the horse, it was the time of their life.

References

- https://www.78rpmcommunity.com/2018/11/15/charles-nat-star-a-life-in-music/
- Other Voices: Hidden Histories of Liverpool's Popular Music Scenes, 1930s-1970s by Michael Brocken
- Peter Faint Jack Hylton
- Sid Phillips Special - Alan Dell's Dance Band Days - 1989

Appendix 7 - Archer Street

In this book I have explained how the sons of immigrants became some of the best known bandleaders in the Golden Age of Dance Bands.

Growing up in tight knit communities, those who took up a musical instrument would have had the opportunity laid out in front of them to form small bands with their co-religionists, and even earn good money accompanying silent films at their local cinema. It is likely that their contacts within the communities would have helped them make their first steps beyond the environs of Bethnal Green and similar 'shtetls'.

For those living in London, especially East London, there was a further route that many could go down. Ronnie Scott (Ronald Schatt) said that Jews who wanted to play music travelled from the

East End to the West End, and for many of them, Jew and non-Jew the place they gravitated to was Archer Street.

Here is an abridged story of Archer Street from John Williamson of the University of Glasgow in an article he co-wrote for the Musicians Union archive:

Archer Street in London is a narrow back street in Soho which became known as a meeting point for the West End musicians during the 1920s and the days of mass unemployment in the 1930s. The reasons that Archer Street became the hub for musicians (rather than, for example, nearby Denmark Street which was the home of music shops and music publishers) was down to its proximity to work places (nearby theatres and clubs) and places to drink and socialise.

While the abundance of tea rooms, pubs and members' clubs in the area undoubtedly contributed to its popularity with musicians, its popularity as a gathering point with musicians stemmed from the 1920s, when the number of musicians working in nearby theatres (The Apollo and The Lyric both had the stage doors which opened into Archer Street) made it an obvious congregation point.

London Orchestral Organisation

While the London Orchestral Association had been absorbed into the Musicians' Union in the 1921 merger, it had retained both its premises and identity as well as retaining a considerable influence on the London Branch of the Union. Its (LOA) headquarters was in Archer Street in the West End of London and was generally referred to as 'the Club', because this is where musicians would go between a matinee and an evening performance in the many theatres nearby, or to find a deputy, or just to meet friends and colleagues. In the main meeting room there was a bar where tea, coffee and snacks could be bought. It also had a licence to sell alcohol which attracted a good deal more custom in the first decades of the 20th century when many musicians, particularly woodwind, brass and percussion players, were quite heavy drinkers. Downstairs there were washing facilities and changing rooms. On the walls there were racks where members requiring a deputy could leave a request, perhaps, 'Joe Bloggs needs 2nd clarinet for evening performance, Tuesday 23rd, 7.30 Her Majesties

However, it was perhaps the exclusive nature of the LOA and their initial reluctance to admit members of the jazz/ dance bands that were becoming popular in the 1920s that meant these musicians were forced to meet outside or nearby. It was primarily for these musicians that Archer Street became what Bill Kirkpatrick, writing in the Musician (June 1993) describes as "a sort of dance band musicians' Labour Exchange."

Labour Exchange

"All the smart hotels, restaurants and clubs were bringing in new style jazz/dance bands. Where there was a firm business investment, regular bands were employed on a full time basis but there was also a great deal of part-time promotion which used players on a casual basis. The old music hall players were not, on the whole, well suited to the new style of music and in London, the new school learned by word of mouth that there was a place where musicians gathered in the West End."

Kirkpatrick notes that the "class of the gigs varied widely" with the top end comprising "high society coming out seasons, annual Hunt balls, end of year Oxford functions and the like," which were largely monopolised by the "big household name band leaders," who had their own fixers who organised replacements if they could not do the shows themselves."

By the 1940s Archer Street was "where anyone would go if they wanted to book musicians for a 'gig', or to play on the big liners, which all employed musicians to play at meal times and for dancing, or for the summer seasons in the Holiday Camps," and while Kirkpatrick reveals that while the actual gig booking were often made by phone, the payments were made on Monday afternoons in Archer Street:

"The offices for that process were the doorways of the few shops in the street or one of the scores of cafes in the are. Further down the scale, lots of gigs were booked in the street, with cash paid at the finish of the job."

George Green, a member of the London branch of the Musicians Union who later died as part of the International Brigade during the Spanish Civil War, painted a grim picture in a letter to the Daily Worker in December 1935:

"Archer Street lies within a stone's throw of Piccadilly, at the back of the Lyric Theatre. Here, every day, gather four or five hundred musicians, many employed today but anxious for tomorrow. This is not the Rhondda. Poverty does not show its access so openly. Sometimes a passerby seeing a thronged pavement, will ask if this is a branch of the Stock Exchange. Stranger! This is no Stock Exchange but a slave market, and here the slave who finds no master starves."

Williamson noted that "In the end in 1961 Melody Maker reported that the Police had stopped allowing musicians to gather on Archer Street on Mondays between 2pm and 5pm. By the end of the decade, the Orchestral Association had closed its doors and the number of musicians employed declined as yet another sea-change in music employment and the music business took place in the 1960s. And, though Archer Street survived as a musical hub through the musical changes of the 1920s and 1930s and the societal ones of World War II and its aftermath, the 1960s were a change too far: musical and social changes combined to change the face of not just Archer Street, but Soho more generally."

King Street Blues: Jazz and the Left in Britain in the 1930s – 1940s mentioned Archer Street: "Just before the war a young Mass-Observer, Hugh Clegg, was mingling with London's dance band players at their Archer Street meeting ground. As usual the street was buzzing, for, with its cafés, pubs, Musicians' Union office and scores of nearby clubs and theatres, it provided the capital's musicians with both an out-of-hours rendezvous and an informal labour exchange. "

An article published in the Melody Maker in 1935 labelled Archer Street as the "Street of Hope". In many other instances this informal network allowed musicians to find employment, thus it could significantly help those entering into London's music scene from outside. For instance, in 1929 Leslie Thompson arrived in London, he was out of work and so he went to Archer Street. The first thing that surprised him was that the street was so crowded that it was almost impossible to walk. Thompson did not know anybody, and was the only black person there. He was even more stupefied when a man came to him asking where he was from and what instrument he played. Eventually, that day he found his first job in London playing in a band that performed at a Jewish wedding.

Hanging Out

A further description of Archer Street was written by Ben Aaronovitch.

Back in the old days, my dad and his mates used to hang out on Archer Street , where the Musicians Union used to be, in the hope of getting work. I'd always imagined it as little knots of musicians dotted along the pavement .

Then I saw a photograph which showed the street awash with men in pork-pie hats and Burton suits toting their instruments around like unemployed Mafiosi. It got so crowded and competitive, my dad said, that bands would have secret hand gestures to communicate across the crowd, sliding fist for a trombonist, flat hand, palm down, for a drummer, fluttering fingers for a cornet or a trumpet .

That way you could stay friendly with your mates in the crowd even while undercutting them for a gig at the Savoy or the Café de Paris. My dad said you could have walked down Archer Street and assembled two full orchestras, a big band and still have enough bodies left for a couple of quartets.

An Indiscreet Side to Soho by Stanley Jackson further backs up this informal even anarchic side to the street. Jackson stated "Your music professional has little sense of time. He will stand about Archer Street for hours on end and then adjourn to the little club or café for a chat or a drink. […] It is not time wasted, however. The musician's grapevine in Archer Street grows just as energetically as that of the waiters in Old Compton Street. He hears that there may be an opening for a sax with Jack Payne or that a new bottle party is opening in Kingly Street on Thursday and that the piano player has let them down. He is in no hurry to tie himself down to regular work. A "gig" suits him better because he will not pay income tax on it. It is impossible to stand about for more than an hour without hearing some hard-luck story from a fellow-pro who has had a streak of ill-fortune. Big talk

Anti-Semitism

It is interesting to note that that with this competition for jobs anti-Semitism showed its face as suggested in *A Weapon in the Struggle The Cultural History of Jazz and the Left in Britain in the 1930s 1940s*.

This states that "the Jewish presence was strongly marked in the British dance bands, where among the Ambrose sidemen alone there was a trumpeter son of a Canadian rabbi, a drummer specialising in 'Yiddisher' comedy numbers and a saxophonist who later recorded an album of Jewish party tunes. On Archer Street that presence met with a certain amount of anti-Semitic feeling and it may be that the hostility of some conventional musicians for dance-band players was similarly affected.

Summary

There can be no doubt that Archer Street played its part in Jewish History, if only a bit part. At a time when the sons of immigrants were looking to find their place in British Society, it will have been a place where they coud make new contacts outside their ethnicity.

Bibliography

https://www.muhistory.com/from-the-archive-4-archer-street-london/
Moon Over Soho: The Second Rivers of London novel By Ben Aaronovitch
A Weapon in the Struggle The Cultural History of t... 7 King Street
Blues Jazz and the Left in Britain in the 1930s 1940s

Appendix 8 - Jewish BritJazz

After all that, a footnote from my book *The Definitive Guide to Jewish Miscellany and Trivia.*

Despite Reithian influences, and despite a ban on American jazz musicians brought about by the Musicians' Union, jazz became the music of choice for young people throughout Britain.

Young Brits had been introduced to the music of Benny Goodman, Glen Miller and the like during the war. Merchant sailors would call into ports such as Liverpool with a steady supply of jazz, rhythm and blues gramophone records, and in the UK there was a brief flowering of jazz, with such luminaries as Chris Barber, Acker Bilk, and Kenny Ball.

There was a Jewish element. Clarinetists/bandleaders such as Sid Phillips were already going down the route of Trad Jazz, and Jewish musicians were playing in jazz bands.

Perhaps one of the greatest influences on post-war British jazz was Ronnie Scott. Born, yes you guessed it, in the East End of London in Aldgate in 1927, Ronald Schatt loved jazz from an early age and was playing in jazz clubs from around 1943.

He played the saxophone, a talent that was to stand him in good stead when he played the saxophone solo in *Lady Madonna* by the Beatles, and in the early days he found work with such as Bert Ambrose. He would work on cruise liners in the early days so as to go to New York and visit the various jazz nightclubs to drink in the culture.

He played jazz all his life, but was best known for his nightclub in London, which opened in 1959 after the Musicians' Union ban had ended. He was able to showcase a constant stream of American musicians, including Stan Getz and Ella Fitzgerald, to name but two.

One person who played regularly at Ronnie Scott's was George Melly, jazz singer, arts critic and columnist, whose only link with Judaism was that he had a Jewish mother (Maud) who according to Melly was a big fan of gefilte fish.

One of the musicians that played with Melly was Ron Rubin (left, above), also from Liverpool, a little known but important character in British jazz – one of those British Jewish Musicians that were around in many bands in the fifties, such as Benny Green.

Of the Jewish musicians who played their part in the jazz revival, perhaps the best known was Monty Sunshine, who played in the Chris Barber Band. Born in 1928, the son of a tailor from Stepney, he was best known for his clarinet solo on the track *Petite Fleur*, a million seller in 1959.

Bibliography/sources

I have always tried to ensure that the information comes from at least two sources, and in many cases there are literally dozens of sources.

However, there is a dearth of information about some individuals, and some information, especially in the obituaries, is slightly suspect. An example is Ambrose's gambling, which was massive, but which is a tale here and a tale there.

There is a paucity of information about how they felt about their roots, and sometimes about where they were buried.

I have used photos from Wikimedia Commons extensively, or asked permission to use photos.

Thanks to John Williamson of the University of Glasgow to use his article for the musicians Union about Archer Street.

Here is my bibliography, full of links. Of course over a period of time many of them will become inactive, but the truth is still out there. Where the main source is *Wikipedia* or the JC Archives or Newspaper Archives I have not always included it in the bibliography.

In particular:

1. Photo of Lyons Tea House

This photograph was scanned and released by the Imperial War Museum on the IWM Non Commercial Licence. The image was catalogued by the IWM as created for the Ministry of Information, which was dissolved in 1946. Consequently, the image and faithful reproductions are considered Crown Copyright, now expired as the photograph was taken prior to 1 June 1957.

2. Geraldo on Tour

As above.

In some cases photos are so widely distributed as to make it impossible to find out who the copyright owner is, and as such are obviously in the public domain.

Occasionally I can see who is the copyright owner but cannot trace them, so I have just recognised their copyright. If they want to contact me, I'll be happy to withdraw the photo.

I used Alan Dell's Radio 2 "The Golden Age of Dance Bands", especially some of the anecdotes, quite a bit. A great resource.

General
- Other Voices: Hidden Histories of Liverpool's Popular Music Scenes, 1930s-1970s by Michael Brocken
- https://www.telegraph.co.uk/culture/culturenews/8528283/Now-thats-what-I-call-chutzpah-the-Jewish-contribution-to-the-entertainment-business.html
- Talking Swing: The British Big Bands by Sheila Tracy
- https://www.muhistory.com/contact-us/1931-1940/
- Soul Trains by Larry Portis
- http://www.themeister.co.uk/dixie/british_dance_bands.htm
- http://holocaustmusic.ort.org/politics-and-propaganda/third-reich/jazz-under-the-nazis/
- Shuldman, K., 2005. Jazz Survivor: The Story of Louis Bannet, Horn Player of Auschwitz, London & Portland,
- http://www.goon.org/usgoons/ellington.htm
- http://michaelcooper.org.uk/C/benny.htm (Benny Freedman)
- King Street Blues Jazz and the Left in Britain in the 1930s 1940s

Ambrose
- https://www.theguardian.com/music/2010/jan/14/pre-rock-popular-music

- http://www.mgthomas.co.uk/dancebands/Musicians/Musicia nPages/Ambrose.htm
- Post-World War II jazz in Britain: Venues and Values 19451970 Williams, KA
- http://hdl.handle.net/10026.1/4429
- http://www.mgthomas.co.uk/dancebands/Musicians/Musicia nPages/Ambrose.htm
- Don't Fuss, Mr Ambrose. Billy Amstell

Lew Stone
- http://www.r2ok.co.uk/stone1.htm
- http://www.lewstone.co.uk/chapters.htm
- https://www.allmusic.com/artist/lew-stone-mn0000822532 (Stone tales over from Fox)
- https://enacademic.com/dic.nsf/enwiki/5028924 (Leo Fuld)
- Blood, Sweat, and Toil: Remaking the British Working Class, 1939-1945 By Geoffrey G. Field

Harry Roy

- https://www.jewishlivesproject.com/profiles/harry-roy

- Talking Swing: The British Big Bands by Sheila Tracey,

- https://www.allmusic.com/artist/harry-roy-mn0000666939/biography

- The Bel Canto Violin: The Life and Times of Alfredo Campoli, 1906-1991 by David Tunley

Geraldo
- https://www.jewishlivesproject.com/profiles/geraldo
- http://www.jazzprofessional.com/big_band_profiles/Geraldo BBP.htm
- Electric Shock: From the Gramophone to the IPhone - 125 Years of Pop Music By Peter Doggett (other "latin" bandleaders.

- Talking Swing: The British Big Bands by Sheila Tracy

Lipton
- Lipton: The Palgrave Dictionary of Anglo-Jewish History

Nat Temple
- http://www.jfpd.co.uk/nattemple/nat01.htm
- R. F. Schwartz, How Britain Got the Blues: the Transmission and Reception of American Blues Style in the United Kingdom p. 28.

Woolf Phillips

Alien invasions: the British Musicians' Union and foreign musicians Citation for published version: Cloonan, M & Brennan, M 2013, 'Alien invasions: the British Musicians' Union and foreign musicians', Popular Music, vol. 32, no. 2, pp. 277-295.

Stanley Black
- https://www.theguardian.com/news/2002/dec/03/guardianobituaries
- https://www.telegraph.co.uk/news/obituaries/1414500/Stanley-Black.html

Joe Loss
- http://www.45-rpm.org.uk/dirj/joel.htm
- The Dance Band Era – Albert McCarthy Spring Books 1971

Maurice Winnick, Bert Firman, Phil Moss
- Oxford Companion to Popular Music (1991) Editors: Rubinstein, W., Jolles, Michael A. (Eds.)
- https://www.theguardian.com/news/1999/apr/21/guardianobituaries1
- https://www.allmusic.com/artist/bert-firman-mn0001926011/biography
- https://www.telegraph.co.uk/news/obituaries/1438245/Woolf-Phillips.html

- http://www.redhotjazz.com/rhapsody.html
- Phil Moss: Manchester's Dancing Years

Johnny Rosen, Nat Bookbinder
- Jack Hylton by Pete Faint
- Harry Francis - Jazz Development in Britain 1924—1974 (http://www.jazzprofessional.com/Main/welcome.html)
- https://wmag.culturewarrington.org/2019/10/11/herbert-greaves-and-the-casino-club/
- Harry Leader
- http://www.mastersofmelody.co.uk/harryleader.htm

Sidney Simone
- Billboard April 22 1995 Obituary
- Photo Jewish Chronicle Archive

Lew Davis
- http://www.r2ok.co.uk/davis01.htm

Other
- http://www.themeister.co.uk/dixie/british_dance_bands.htm
- Going to the Palais: A Social And Cultural History of Dancing and Dance ...- James Nott
- Dance Halls: Towards an Architectural and Spatial History, c. 1918–65 James Nott. Copyright Cambridge University Press
- Benny Loban This is from a biography written in the Vintage Dance Band Website - http://www.r2ok.co.uk/loban.htm

-

Printed in Great Britain
by Amazon